THE PRINCIPLES OF ASTROLOGY

THEORETICAL AND APPLIED

By

CHARLES E. O. CARTER, B.A.

PRESIDENT OF THE ASTROLOGICAL LODGE OF
THE THEOSOPHICAL SOCIETY

AUTHOR OF
" AN ENCYCLOPAEDIA OF PSYCHOLOGICAL ASTROLOGY "
" THE ZODIAC AND THE SOUL "
" SYMBOLIC DIRECTIONS IN MODERN ASTROLOGY "
" SEVEN GREAT PROBLEMS OF ASTROLOGY "
" THE ASTROLOGICAL ASPECTS "
" SOME PRINCIPLES OF HOROSCOPIC DELINEATION "

BEL AIR MARYLAND
ASTROLOGY CLASSICS
207 VICTORY LANE

ISBN-10   1 933303 26 3
ISBN-13   978 1 933303 26 0

The publisher wishes to thank
ROBERT P. BLASCHKE
EARTHWALK SCHOOL OF ASTROLOGY
for bringing this book to his attention.

*Charles Carter was born at Parkstone, Dorset,
on 31 January 1887, at 11:01 pm.*

He died on 4 October, 1968, 4:30 pm, London.

Published 2009 by
Astrology Classics

The publishing division of
The Astrology Center of America
207 Victory Lane
Bel Air MD 21014

On line at **AstroAmerica.com**

FOREWORD

THE present work is designed to give a clear and concise presentation of the essential facts of modern Astrology.

A good deal of experience in teaching the average beginner has convinced me that, while there are several text-books suitable for the use of the more advanced student or of a novice who has the advantage of personal tuition, the majority are either too prolix or too condensed for one who is compelled to be his own instructor. Moreover, Astrology is now to some extent in the melting-pot : on the one hand, many new ideas are being introduced ; on the other, statistical research, such as earlier astrologers could not carry out for lack of sufficient data, has cast considerable doubt on the validity of portions of the rather incoherent mass of tradition that till recent years represented astrological science.

The beginner does not wish to be confronted with controversial matters, however attractive he may find them later. He requires, firstly, a statement of what may be regarded as known astrological facts ; and secondly, an explanation as to how these facts affect human life. It is this that I have aimed at giving him.

An endeavour is made not to neglect the theoretical aspects of Astrology, for the modern student dislikes what appear to him as isolated statements, and looks for a logical and synthetic aspect to our teaching, without, of course, wishing to plunge at the outset into metaphysical speculation.

I trust that the Index will be of considerable use in practice, since it should enable the student to find readily those passages that deal with any matter that may trouble him.

Finally, I would express my sincere hope that this book may be of some value in assisting its readers to grasp something of the true nature and worth of astrological science, both in the commonest and the most sublime aspects of human life. Those who have realized what this may mean to the individual are reluctant to set any bounds to their estimate of the beneficial effects that its universal recognition, in a proper form, would mean to the human race.

CHARLES E. O. CARTER

February, 1925.

FOREWORD TO THE SECOND EDITION

This edition represents a careful revision of the former text, and, besides many minor alterations, some substantial additions have been made, chiefly in Chapter Two. Here, in particular, a table of Zone Times has been inserted.

Brevity is necessary in order to keep to a price that all can pay, but I have tried to avoid any sacrifice of lucidity, or, within the scope of the book, of completeness.

My chief desire has been to keep a sense of proportion, throwing the main principles into bold relief, for, if these are once comprehended, the particulars will be easily assimilated.

Chapter Ten has been augmented with sections on Symbolic Directions and on Rectification.

It would hardly be human to feel no pleasure in contemplating the many friends this work has made for me in the most diverse parts of the world which I can never hope to visit in the flesh. I trust that this fresh edition will continue the activities of its forerunner and spread the wonderful illumination of astrological knowledge ever further afield.

CHARLES E. O. CARTER

October, 1930.

FOREWORD TO THE THIRD EDITION

THE publication of a third edition of this work has enabled me to make a careful revision of the whole, to make certain alterations in the text and a few additions which will, I hope, be of the nature of improvements. On the whole, however, the book remains unchanged.

CHARLES E. O. CARTER

August, 1939.

THE PRINCIPLES OF ASTROLOGY

CONTENTS

CHAPTER ONE

CHAPTER TWO

CHAPTER THREE

CONTENTS

CHAPTER FOUR

CHAPTER FIVE

CHAPTER SIX

CHAPTER SEVEN

CONTENTS

CHAPTER EIGHT

PAGE

CHAPTER NINE

CHAPTER TEN

Section 1. Classification of Factors.
     2. Transits, Lunations, Revolutions, and the
        Diurnal Horoscope.
     3. Secondary Directions.
     4. Primary Directions.
     5. Symbolic Directions.
     6. Rectification.

CHAPTER ELEVEN

Section 1. Horary Questions.
     2. Elections.

CHAPTER TWELVE

THE PRINCIPLES OF ASTROLOGY

CHAPTER ONE

ASTROLOGY AND ITS SUBJECT-MATTER

§ 1. INTRODUCTORY

ASTROLOGY is the science of certain cryptic relations between the celestial bodies and terrestrial life.

Natal Astrology is the study of these relations in regard to human life.

Furthermore, Astrology is a practical science; for it teaches us how to apply the information that it imparts to our personal and social life. Also, it is an Art, for the delineation of the Nativity, or Horoscope of Birth, calls into play faculties allied to the artistic.

The uses of Astrology are manifold, and its rope is limited only by the bounds of human life in its widest extent. The following aspects of the science may be mentioned :

Philosophical : It endeavours to set forth a coherent and scientifically verifiable scheme of cosmic manifestation.

Ethical : It traces the interactions between the Cosmos and the human mind and soul, and studies the true nature of what are called good and evil. It gives understanding of ourselves and others, and consequently broadens the sympathies and enlarges the outlook.

Spiritual and Religious : It endeavours to understand the essential nature of the divine ordinances and the ministers of divine power, in so far as is humanly possible.

Practical : By explaining the operations of cosmic laws it enables us to adapt our lives to them, and to advise and assist others to make the most of their lives, without waste of time and effort.

On the other hand, it must be borne in mind that our knowledge of Astrology is very far from complete. It is still studied by comparatively few, and it is overlaid with the growth of centuries of ignorance and charlatanism.

Astrology does not involve any form of psychism, and is founded upon mathematical and astronomical data, interpreted according to general principles.

It would be premature, at this stage and in a work of this nature, to discuss whether the heavenly bodies affect us directly as causative agents, or whether there is simply a correspondence between their motions and positions and the natures and destinies of human races and individuals. There may be truth in both views.

Practical experiment will soon convince the most sceptical that the bodies of the solar system indicate, if they do not actually produce, changes in :

1. Our minds.
2. Our feelings and emotions.
3. Our physical bodies.
4. Our external affairs and relationships with the world at large.

Astrology studies, as its subject-matter, four chief categories :

1. The Sun, Moon, and Planets.
2. The Zodiac.
3. The Houses of the Horoscope.
4. The Planetary Aspects.

We may mention, further, the Fixed Stars, whose value, at least so far as the individual is concerned, is questioned by many, and Sensitive Points, which, except the Part of Fortune, are beyond the scope of an introductory work.

In this chapter it is proposed to explain in a general sense what each of these four categories is, treating them in detail in subsequent chapters.

§ 2

The Sun, Moon, and Planets comprise the main elements of our Solar System, or Sun-System. The Sun is a fixed star, like others that one sees on a clear night ; and all the Planets, of which the Earth is one, revolve round it in their " orbits ", while most, if not all, planets have satellites or moons which revolve round them. The earth has one satellite—our Moon ; the satellites of the other planets possess no known astrological importance. The Fixed Stars are immensely farther from us than even the most distant planet.

The Sun is indicated by the symbol ☉ and the Moon by ☽, and the planets and their symbols are as follows, counting from the Sun outwards :

Mercury	☿
Venus	♀
(The Earth)	—
Mars	♂
Jupiter	♃
Saturn	♄
Uranus	♅
Neptune	♆
Pluto ... (not yet determined)	[♇]

The Earth can hardly be studied astrologically, for the reason that its value must necessarily be the same for all of us. It is our station at which we receive the rays of the other planets as they circle around the Sun with it, in ever-changing mutual relations.

Uranus and Neptune were discovered in modern times; the others have been known from remote ages. Pluto was discovered in 1930.

The Sun and Moon are commonly called the *Lights* or *Luminaries*.

Venus and Jupiter are traditionally called the lesser and greater *benefics*, and Mars and Saturn the lesser and greater *malefics*.

By the adherents of some schools of thought, it has been objected that it is incorrect to apply these terms to any planets. Nevertheless they are in practice highly convenient. When well placed the benefics indicate easy fortunes and the more social and brighter virtues ; the malefics, success by hard work and the harder and more worldly-useful qualities. Under serious afflictions the benefics cause the less grave misfortunes and such failings as indolence and extravagance, which make a man his own enemy rather than actively harmful to others ; the malefics in such circumstances may occasion dangerous conditions and a very unfortunate or even malignant disposition.[1]

Uranus and Neptune incline somewhat to the malefic character. The Sun, Moon, and Mercury depend greatly for the nature of their action on their special positions in each horoscope. They are termed *Neutrals*. The nature of Pluto is still a matter for investigation.

§ 3. THE SIGNS OF THE ZODIAC

Astrological philosophy teaches that visible Nature (at least so far as we are able to observe it) arises from the inter-action of what are called the four *Elements*[2] a (or Triplici-ties), symbolically named Fire, Air, Earth, and Water, and the three *Qualities* (Quadruplicities) or modes of action, named the Cardinal, Fixed, and Mutable. These seven prin-ciples are cosmic, or universal, whereas the Sun, Moon, and Planets are of course finite existences within our Solar Sys-tem. We have no reason to suppose that other solar sys-tems are counterparts of our own : indeed, it is certain that they are not. But there is no reason to suppose that the Elements and Qualities are merely local.

The *Zodiac* is the pathway of the Sun, Moon, and plan-ets, and lies like a belt round the earth. It is invisible, and we can only detect its position by noticing where the plan-ets are at night, just as one can trace the course of a distant

---

[1] Such statements as the above may sound fatalistic. It is impossible, at every stage in a text-book, to guard against expressions which may to some ears have this implication, but the reader is referred to the last chapter for a note on this problem and its relations to Astrology.

[2] Not, of course, to be confused with the chemical elements of modern physics.

road at night by watching the lights of the traffic passing along it. The fixed stars are not limited to the zodiac ; as we can see for ourselves they are scattered over the entire sky. Some of course lie in the Zodiac, such as Antares, Aldebaran, Castor and Pollux, and Regulus.

At all times and places half the zodiac lies above the horizon and half below.

It is divided into twelve signs, each containing 30 degrees (written °), making 360 degrees in all.

The Latin and English names of these twelve signs, with their symbols, are as follows :

1. Aries the Ram .... ♈
2. Taurus the Bull .... ♉
3. Gemini the Twins .... ♊
4. Cancer the Crab .... ♋
5. Leo the Lion .... ♌
6. Virgo the Maiden .... ♍
7. Libra the Scales .... ♎
8. Scorpio the Scorpion .... ♏
9. Sagittarius the Archer .... ♐
10. Capricorn the He-Goat .... ♑
11. Aquarius the Water Bearer .... ♒
12. Pisces the Fishes .... ♓

Now this division into twelve arises from the fact that the zodiac is constructed from the elements and qualities. Four signs belong to each of the three qualities, and one of each group of four belongs to each element. Thus :

	Fire.	Water.	Air.	Earth.
Cardinal	Aries	Cancer	Libra	Capricorn
Fixed	Leo	Scorpio	Aquarius	Taurus
Mutable	Sagittarius	Pisces	Gemini	Virgo

The significance of the elements and qualities is explained in Chapter Four.

Further, all odd signs (i.e., fire and air) are called *Positive*, and all even signs (earth and water) are called *Negative*.

The positive signs are related to the masculine, outgoing, or aggressive side of Nature ; the negative to the feminine, indrawn, or protective side. The former express themselves fully and freely on whatever line may be theirs ; the latter are usually reserved and receptive.

Sign-Rulership

The planets and signs are related by what is known as sign-rulership, each planet ruling two signs, called by some astrologers its " Houses " , although this term is ambiguous, since the word " house " has a special and altogether different meaning in Astrology, and it is equally easy to speak of a planet's sign, which is not open to misunderstanding. The Sun rules a positive and the Moon a negative sign, and each planet rules one of each.

This allocation of rulership is not arbitrary, as we shall see if we arrange the signs in two columns in their natural order, beginning with Leo at the head of the left-hand column, and travelling down that column and then up the next, so as to end with Cancer. We see that the signs then appear in pairs, each pair being ruled by one planet, while the planets are in the order of their distance from the Sun. Thus :

| Leo | Cancer | ruled by Sun and Moon respectively. |
| Virgo | Gemini | ruled by Mercury. |

Libra	Taurus	ruled by Venus.
Scorpio	Aries	ruled by Mars.
Sagittarius	Pisces	ruled by Jupiter.
Capricorn	Aquarius	ruled by Saturn.

Uranus, Neptune and Pluto have no definite rulership, although the first has points of resemblance to Scorpio and Aquarius, and the second is, perhaps, even more like Pisces in some characteristics.

Furthermore, each body has an *Exaltation*, or sign in which it is specially strong and favourable. These are :

The Sun .... Aries   *The Moon* ...... Taurus
Mercury .... Virgo   *Venus* .... Pisces
Mars .... Capricorn   *Jupiter* .... Cancer
Saturn .... Libra

The signs opposite its own signs are called the *Detriments* of a planet, and that opposite its exaltation its *Fall*. In these it is weak and its power perverted. In its own sign a body is strong, and in its exaltation it is also strong, and its action improved.

Two bodies each in the sign of the other are said to be in *mutual reception*, which is considered harmonious. A planet is said to *dispose* of bodies placed in its signs. Thus planets in Aries would be disposed of by Mars, and Mars is then called their *dispositor*.

The Ruler or Lord of the Horoscope

It is considered that one planet (or the Sun or Moon) in a special sense stands in the horoscope for the *native* or person for whom the nativity is erected, while the rest of the nativity represents aspects of his life which are external to him, as, for example, his friends, occupation, wife, children, and so on.

This body is called the Ruler or Lord of the Horoscope, and it is to it that astrologers refer when they call a person a " Martian " or " Uranian ", or otherwise as the case may be.[1] It is usually the ruler of the 1st House,[2] but probably not invariably so, for if that body is very weak, whereas anther is much stronger, as by rising near the asc.,[2] with strong aspects (especially to the Sun, Moon or Mercury), or by being on the M.C., it may apparently become the ruler. It is then the representative of the personal self, much as the asc.[2] and 1st house[2] generally are, and in a certain sense all the rest of the map may be regarded as external to it. Thus, if Mars afflicts the ruler we regard this as indicating that Martian matters are inimical to the native, and so on.

But in a deeper sense the entire nativity represents the native.

The signs start from the vernal equinox, or 0° Aries, which is the point in the zodiac at which the Sun, on about the 21st of March in each year, crosses the celestial equator and passes into north declination.

We may now explain four terms which even those who have made some progress in astrological studies do not always clearly understand :

Celestial Latitude[3] is the distance of a body north or south from the centre line of the zodiac. If we liken the zodiac to a path along which the planets travel, the line down the centre of that path is the *Ecliptic*, and all deviation north or south of this is latitude.

---

[1] When we speak of a person by the name of a sign, as an Arietic person, a Leo, and so on, we refer (or ought to refer) to the rising sign.

[2] To be explained in Section 4.

[3] Termed *Celestial* latitude in contradistinction to geographical.

Celestial Longitude[1] is simply the distance of a body from 0° Aries, the beginning of the zodiac, stated in degrees and minutes (1 minute = 1/60 of a degree) of the signs. This is the usual manner of describing the position of a planet. We say, for example, that a body is in the first degree of Gemini, meaning it is two signs, or 60 degrees, from 0° Aries.

Latitude and Longitude thus enable us to define the position in the sky of a body by measuring along the ecliptic and up and down from it.

We now come to two analogous measures related to the celestial equator, which is a projection of the earth's equator on to the heavens.

Right Ascension is measured along the equator from 0° Aries.

Declination is measured up and down (north and south) from the equator.

By this measure we define any point in the sky in relation to the celestial equator.

Longitude and Declination are the two most important measures from the standpoint of Astrology. Right Ascension and latitude are only used in connection with certain kinds of prognostic work.

Other divisions of the signs besides that into degrees are employed astrologically, of which the one most frequently mentioned is that into thirds, of 10° each, called *Decans* or *Decanates*.

According to the Hindu system the first decanate of each sign is of the nature of that sign in its purity ; the second decanate has a sub-influence of the next sign of the same element, and the last decanate a sub-influence of the last sign of that element.

For example :

0°—10° ♈ has a subinfluence of ♈;
10°—20° ♈ has a subinfluence of ♌ ;
20°—30° ♈ has a subinfluence of ♐.

The Beginner should thoroughly master the primary characteristics of the signs before troubling about the secondary.

The Signs of the Zodiac are not the same as the *Constellations* (groups of fixed stars) that bear the same names. At one time they were coincident, but, owing to

---

[1] Termed *Celestial* longitude in contradistinction to geographical.

what is called the precession of the equinoxes, this is no longer the case, so that, for example, the two well-known stars in the constellation Gemini, Castor and Pollux, are in the sign Cancer.

§ 4. THE HOUSES OF THE HOROSCOPE

These result from a division into twelve of the visible and invisible sky at any place and time. The sky above the horizon is divided into six sections, and similarly the sky beneath the horizon. These twelve sections are the familiar divisions of the horoscopical figure.

This division of the sky cuts the zodiac into twelve sections, which are not necessarily coincident with the twelve signs, and indeed in these latitudes never are. It is as if one watched a moving road-way through a window divided into six sections by fixed iron bars. The moving roadway might be itself divided into twelve sections (i.e., " signs "), but, as it moved, the bars of the window would cut it into sections that would rarely coincide with the divisions of the roadway itself.

Moreover, the twelve houses do not (except at the equator) contain exactly 30° each, but vary in this respect, as we shall see later.

We, so to speak, watch the moving sky, which contains the zodiac and planets, through the bars of the houses, which remain immovable, while the sky appears to sweep from east to west.

And while the sky sweeps round *from east to west* once in every twenty-four hours, this movement being caused by the rotation of the Earth on its axis, the sun, moon, and planets, owing to their real motion round the sun, gradually move *from west to east* through the signs of the zodiac.

The beginner must get a clear idea of the distinction

23

between the signs, which are, so to speak, part of the sky itself and move with it, although invisible, and the houses, which as explained are, from the standpoint of the observer, stationary.

The houses are not named, but are known by their numbers, beginning with the 1st, immediately below the eastern horizon, and then following round as shown in the diagram on page 26.

The *cusp* of a house is its beginning, the dividing line between it and the preceding house. These are the " spokes " of the horoscopical wheel shown opposite.

The cusp of the 1st house, or eastern horizon, is called the *Ascendant* (abbr. asc.), and the cusp of the 10th, or zenith, is called the *Midheaven* or M.C. (from Latin, *medium coeli*). The cusp of the 7th is sometimes called the descendant, and the cusp of the 4th the nadir or I.C. (from Latin, *imum coeli*).

The 1st, 4th, 7th, and 10th houses, corresponding to the cardinal signs, are called *angular*.

The 2nd, 5th, 8th, and 11th, corresponding to the fixed signs, are called *succeedent*.

The 3rd, 6th, 9th and 12th, corresponding to the mutables, are called *cadent*.

Logically, however, there is no reason why new names should be used, for the houses correspond in nature to their respective signs. They are not classified according to element at all, but in this respect also there is no reason why the 1st, 5th, and 9th, for example, should not be called "fiery" houses, corresponding as they do to the fiery signs.

In a general sense the signs are said to relate to character, the houses to environment. Thus, Taurus (the 2nd *sign*) gives a love of comfort ; the 2nd *house*, ruling possessions, bestows the means of gratifying it. In actual practice there seems little difference between a sign-position and the corresponding house-position so far as their relation to character and environment are concerned.

The houses are said to be *ruled* by the planet which rules the sign on its cusp, or, if a sign is intercepted,[1] its ruler is *part-ruler* of the house. This is styled *accidental rulership*, because it varies with each horoscope. The planet ruling the sign corresponding to a house is called the *essential or natural ruler* of that house. Thus, Venus is essential ruler of the 2nd and 7th, because it rules the 2nd and 7th signs ; but any planet may be their accidental ruler.

The student should now study the diagram or horoscopic form shown on the following page.

A horoscope is a diagram of the heavens erected for any time and place for the purpose of astrological study. A horoscope for a birth-time is called a nativity.

Horoscopes embody the three categories with which we have dealt, viz., the Sun, Moon, and Planets, the Signs, and the Houses.

The form overleaf is not filled in ; it merely gives the houses.

If the student wishes, he can cut out two forms similar to this, using one (preferably transparent) to represent the houses, and the other the signs, the symbols of which he would then insert in place of the numbers of the houses in the first one. He can then pin the " houses " on to the " signs ", and, keeping the first fixed, can revolve the other beneath it in the same direction as that traversed by the hands of a clock. It can then be clearly seen how the signs sweep through the houses, so that at one time Aries may be " rising ", i.e., occupying the asc. or cusp of the 1st house, and

---

[1] See pages 39, 40.

afterwards Taurus, and so on. If he further divides the signs into thirtieth parts to represent degrees, he can see which degree of which sign is on any cusp at any moment.

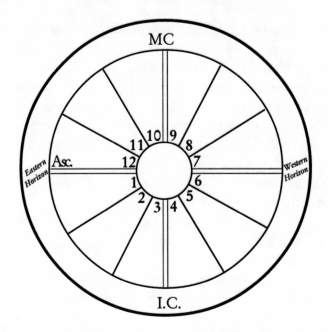

Furthermore, the planets may be inserted on the " signs " diagram, each in its own sign and degree, and they will then be carried round with the signs ; but to complete the model it would be necessary for them to move slightly (about one degree a day in the case of the Sun) in an anti-clockwise direction through the degrees of the signs, this being their proper motion.

Those to whom the astronomical facts on which Astrology rests are not too clear may find some such model as this useful at this stage.

ASTROLOGY AND ITS SUBJECT-MATTER

§ 5. THE ASPECTS

The Sun, Moon, and Planets are said to be *in aspect* with one another when placed at definite distances from each other in the zodiac, such distances, or aspects, being measured in degrees.

By dividing the 360° of the zodiac by 2, 4 and 8, we obtain the so-called *malefic* aspects which indicate opposing or inharmonious influences. By dividing it by 3, 6 and 12, we obtain the *benefic* or harmonious aspects. By dividing it by 2½, 5, 10 and 20, we obtain a series of minor aspects, said to be benefic, which the beginner may disregard.[1]

The aspects and their symbols are as follows :

	Good	Evil
Powerful	Trine, 120° △	Opposition, 180° ☍
	Sextile, 60° ✶	Square, 90° ☐
Weak	Semi-sextile, 30° ⎗	Semi-square, 45° ∠
		Sesquiquadrate, 135° ⚼
		Quincunx, 150° ⚻

By some the opposition is regarded as not necessarily evil, but as indicating two complementary forces that can be harmonized.

The aspects obtained by dividing 360° by five and its derivatives are the Quintile, 72° ; the Biquintile, 144° ; the Decile, 36° ; and the Vigintile, 18°.

The *Conjunction* (symbol ☌) occurs when two bodies are close together in the same sign, or at the end of one and the beginning of the next.

---

[1] This is the usual view, but many students consider this series important.

27

The *Parallel of Declination* occurs when two bodies have the same declination or distance from the celestial equator. Whether both of them are north, both south, or one north and one south, appears immaterial. It is abbreviated as par. dec., par., or simply P.

These two last are good when formed between two benefics, or a benefic and a neutral, and doubtful when formed between benefics and malefics, the former being injured and the latter benefited in such a case. Between malefics and neutrals they are bad, although the student must in such cases pay attention to their respective natures, the sign occupied and other modifying factors. For instance, Sun conjunction Mars is far better than Moon conjunction the same planet, for the Sun is exalted in Aries, the sign of Mars, and so has affinity with the planet, but the Moon is in its fall in Scorpio, the other Martian sign, and so has no favourable affinity with the planet.

Two malefics in conjunction denote a critical feature in the life and character, and need careful study.

Orbs.—It rarely happens that an aspect is exact, that is, that any two bodies are *exactly* in square or trine, or any other aspect. The nearer they are to exactitude the stronger the aspect, but a certain sphere of influence is allowed to each body, called its orb.

Thus, if the Sun were in 0° ♈ and Mars in 0° ♌ they would be 120° apart, and therefore in exact trine. But if they were in 5° ♈ and 10° ♌ respectively, they would still be considered in trine, although 125° apart, because of the orb allowable.

28

It may be said that for a ♂ or ☍ 9° may be allowed; for a △ or □ about 8°; for a ✶, about 7°; for the ∠ and ⚼ about 4°; for a ⚺, a parallel, a ⚻, or a quintile and its cognates, about 1°. A little more may be allowed for the Sun and Moon. For the asc. or M.C., take about 5° as the maximum.

Aspects are ordinarily formed from signs which are themselves in aspect. Thus a body in the beginning of Cancer is in square to one at the beginning of Libra and in trine to one at the beginning of Scorpio. But it would also be in trine to one at the *end* of Libra, although Libra is in square with Cancer. Such aspects are termed *dissociate*, and are often overlooked by beginners. It is probable that they are less powerful than those formed from the correct signs.

The beginner should learn to reckon aspects not by counting from sign to sign, but by noting the signs containing the two bodies he is considering. All signs of the same quality are in square; all of the same element, in trine. Hence bodies in them, if near the same degrees respectively, must also be in the same aspect.

Those who find it easier to reckon by rule of thumb may judge aspects as follows :

Start from the planet that is nearer 0° ♈ and count the signs forward to the sign containing the second body. For each sign take 30°. Thus, if the first planet is in Aries and the second in Virgo we should count five signs — ♉, ♊, ♋, ♌, and ♍, which would equal 150° (5 × 30° = 150°).

Then add the degrees and minutes of the second body to this figure. For example, if it were in 5° 31' ♍ we should get 155° 31'.

From this subtract the degrees and minutes of the first body.

Thus, if this were in 18° 24' ♈ we should say

$$
\begin{array}{r}
155° 31' \\
\textit{Less} \quad 18° 24' \\
\hline
137° 07' \\
\hline
\end{array}
$$

Looking at the table we should find that this is near the sesquiquadrate (135°) and would in fact be within orbs of that aspect, for which we allow, as stated previously, 4°.

A Note on Aspects

Beginners should beware of an automatic classification of aspects into " good " and " bad " without due reference to the more general features of each figure, and, in particular, to the signs and houses occupied by the contacting bodies. This error is common even among comparatively experienced students. The so-called bad aspects are stronger than the good ones, and therefore are potentially more difficult, especially if the more vigorous planets are involved. But, on the other hand, it is quite arguable that, in the case of the less energetic bodies, a square is better than a trine, even if it may not be so " lucky ".

A careful tabulation of many cases of good aspects on the one hand and bad aspects on the other, between the same bodies, has convinced the present writer that there is not always much to choose between them, heretical though this statement unquestionably is.

Undoubtedly the trine and sextile are harmonious contacts. But the maintenance of harmony is not the supreme end of human life, even though without some measure of harmonious adaptation, life would be impossible.

§ 6. MINOR CONSIDERATIONS [1]

Mundane Aspects

These are similar to the foregoing except that they are calculated in terms of *houses*, instead of *signs*. Thus, a planet on the cusp of the 4th would always be square one rising *mundanely*, although not necessarily zodiacally. Often bodies are in good aspect zodiacally and evil aspect mundanely, except on the equator,

---

[1] These may be omitted at the first reading.

where they would always coincide. Their use introduces much difficulty in practical judgment ; and although there is some evidence for their efficacy few students appear to employ them consistently, and the beginner should omit them.

The word " mundane " is often used in Astrology to denote something that has to do with the houses rather than the signs ; indeed, it is often used as the adjective corresponding to the substantive " House ", for which no recognized adjective exists, although some writers use " domal " in this sense, from the Latin *domus*.

The Part of Fortune

At this point mention must be made of what is called the Part of Fortune (symbolized ⊕).

This is a point in the horoscope which is at the same distance from the ascending degree, in either direction, as the Moon is from the Sun. In other words, it is to the asc. as the Moon is to the Sun. If the Sun and Moon are in conjunction, it will be conjunction with the asc. ; if they are in opposition, it will be on the cusp of the 7th house, and so on.

It was believed by old writers, and some moderns, to affect the financial conditions of the native very powerfully. Others have doubted this, and some deny its influence entirely.

The present writer considers that it marks an important centre of interest in the native's life, and, if strong, shows success and honour, and the contrary if weak. But it is very questionable if its action is specifically financial. Thus, in the 3rd house it might show interest in writings and books, but not necessarily gain through literature. If badly afflicted it certainly seems to check the native's general success, as well as affecting the special matters denoted by its house.

Some suggest that it should be reckoned as being at the same distance from the asc. as the Moon was from the Sun at *sunrise* on the day of birth, instead of at the actual time of birth. This may make several degrees' difference, and means that it shows the place of the Moon at sunrise.

Other " Parts " are sometimes used for the planets, all reckoned from the asc. and based on the distance or " elongation " of the planet from the Sun. Other sensitive points or parts are calculated by special rules left to us by seventeenth-century writers such as Gadbury, but none of these merits mention in an introductory work.

The Nodes

The Nodes of the Moon are the points in the ecliptic where ☽ passes from south to north latitude, and the reverse. The Ascending node is called the *Dragon's Head* (symbol ☊) and the Descending node the *Dragon's Tail* (symbol ☋) and they are said to be of the natures, respectively, of Jupiter and Saturn, conferring honour and success or downfall and ruin. They are held to operate only by conjunction. Some writers deny or question their value. Others attach much importance to them, and also recommend using the planetary nodes.

Beginners are advised to defer such investigations to a later stage.

The Grand Trine

It sometimes happens that two bodies are in trine and a third body is in trine with each. Such a configuration was considered very evil by medieval writers and unfortunately this view appears to be often correct. Often there seems to be too great dependence upon others.

We have now completed our survey of all the main objects of astrological study, without, however, entering into the special powers or values of these objects. The beginner is advised thoroughly to master this chapter, including the symbols, the use of which is not only highly convenient, but absolutely essential, inasmuch as they are employed universally in astrological writings. Subsequent chapters, except perhaps the next, which deals with the erection of the horoscope, will be found much easier, involving as they do less memorization.

CHAPTER TWO

THE ERECTION OF THE HOROSCOPE

For this purpose we require the place and time of birth ; an ephemeris (plural, ephemerides), or table of planetary positions, for the year in question ; a Table of Houses for the latitude of the place of birth ; and a horoscopical form.

Raphael's yearly ephemeris includes tables of houses for the latitudes of London, Liverpool and New York. These will serve for all places within a degree or so of these latitudes. Thus, Bath, Bristol, and Reading are practically the same as London, and New York is almost the same as Madrid and Rome.

The erecting, or setting up, of a horoscope involves two operations—inserting the houses, and inserting the planets.

To Insert the Houses

Open the ephemeris for the year of birth and find the pages for the month required. Disregard the upper half of the two pages devoted to that month ; they comprise details not needed at this stage.

Find the day of the month by referring to the first column on the left-hand side of the left-hand page : the numbers therein are the days of the month. The next column shows the days of the week.

The third column is headed *Sidereal Time* (abbreviated S.T.) and contains the S.T. at noon at Greenwich for each day.

Now copy down the S.T. for the *noon first preceding birth*. If the birth-time is p.m. it will be noon of the same day ; if it is a.m. it will be noon of the day before.

Correction One.[1]

To obtain exact results for all horoscopes erected for places east or west of Greenwich a small correction must be made because the S.T. at noon given in the ephemeris is only correct for Greenwich longitude. To effect this correction add 10 seconds to the S.T. at noon at Greenwich for every 15° that the birth-place is west of Greenwich, and subtract the same amount for every 15° that it is east. It is obvious that this correction is negligible for all places in the British Isles and can never amount to more than 2 minutes, which is the correction for 180°.

Now add to the S.T. at noon (corrected as above) the time between that noon and birth.

If the child is born at 4 p.m., you will add four hours ; if at 4 a.m., 16 hours.

In all horoscopes for times during which Summer time was in operation one hour must be deducted at this point, in order to obtain ordinary clock time.

Correction Two.[1]

For every hour thus added to the S.T. at noon add a further ten seconds. This is because the time added is clock-time, and this must be adjusted to make it equal sidereal time.

---

[1]Corrections One and Two may be omitted by beginners.

Correction Three.

This is most important. For every degree of longitude that the place of birth is east of the longitude of standard time for the country[1] in question add four minutes, and for every degree that it is west of the standard longitude, subtract four minutes.

Finally, if your result exceeds 24 hours subtract that number of hours from it.

You now have the S.T. at birth.

Let us work two examples.

Birth is at 3.30 a.m., 2nd January, 1930, at Bournemouth, 2° west longitude (i.e., west of the longitude of Greenwich, which is the standard for Great Britain).

	hrs.	min.	sec.
S.T. at noon on the 1st January, 1930	18	41	39
Correction One—*Add*			1
Add time of birth after noon of 1st	15	30	0
Add Correction Two		2	35
	34	14	15
Subtract 24 hours	24	0	0
	10	14	15
Subtract Correction Three		8	0
	10	6	15

Let us suppose birth took place at the same clock-time, but at New York.

---

[1]See table at end of this Chapter.

We proceed :

	hrs.	min.	sec.
S.T. at noon on the 1st January, 1930	18	41	39
Correction One (New York is 74⁰ west)			50
Add time of birth afternoon of 1st	15	30	0
Add Correction Two		2	35
	34	15	4
Subtract 24 hours	24	0	0
	10	15	4

Add Correction Three, because the long. of New York is 74⁰ w., but the standard longitude for the Atlantic Coast of the U.S.A. is 75⁰w. : so that New York is 1⁰ *east* of its standard meridian 4 0

| | 10 | 19 | 4 |

It will be seen that it is Correction Three which can make the most difference.

Now, whichever of the two foregoing examples you wish to use, turn to the Table of Houses of the latitude required and you will find at the top left-hand corner, left-hand page, the heading " Sidereal Time ", and in the column beneath, the hours, minutes and seconds of S.T. beginning at 0 hr. 0' 0". In this column find the S.T. you require, and opposite it you will find the degrees and signs that at that time, at the latitude in question, occupy the 10th, 11th, 12th, 1st, 2nd, and 3rd house-cusps. Insert these, and opposite them the same degrees of the opposite signs.

You then have your houses completed.

It is a good plan to begin with horoscopes for London, in which case Corrections One and Three do not apply at all. The former is of very little importance for any horoscopes for the British Isles, for it is rare that the time of birth is so accurately recorded that a few seconds matter.[1]

Birth in Southern Latitudes

Here we have two simple additional adjustments. Work exactly as before, but to your answer add 12 hours.

When you insert the degrees and signs on the spokes of the horoscopic figure, use the degrees given in the Table of Houses, but insert the *opposite* signs.

It will be seen that, in some circumstances, the erection of the houses is a matter calling for care, if not for actual skill. But by proceeding step by step, as explained previously, the possibility of error will be greatly reduced. When you have finished your horoscope it is a good plan to glance at the position of the Sun, which must, of course, roughly indicate the time of birth. This serves as a check on any serious error.

To Insert Planets : Birth in England or Scotland

Use the Greenwich time without any adjustment.

The planetary positions are given for noon, and, if the birth is at noon, are simply copied out.

---

[1] So far as nativities are concerned, great mathematical precision is, for this reason, usually mere pedantry. But it may be desired to erect maps for other events (e.g. an accident) when the time is exactly known.

If the birth is before or after noon it is necessary to find their daily motion (given in Raphael's ephemeris, but in any case easily found by subtraction), and then to work out a little sum to find how far they would go in a certain time (i.e., the time before or after noon at which birth took place) in view of the fact that they go so far in the day. With the slower-moving planets this can be seen at a glance, but with the others it must be worked out.

Suppose, for example, birth is at 3 p.m. Jan. 2, 1930, and we want the position of Mars. We see that at noon he was in 3° 3' ♑, and at noon on the next day at 3° 49' ♑. His daily motion = 46'. Then how far will he go in three hours? The answer is 1/8 of 46', or about 6', and we therefore add this to the noon position, and get 3° 9'. If birth were 9 a.m. we should of course *subtract* 6' from the noon position.

The student is advised, however, to use the logarithmic method explained at the end of the ephemeris. Logarithms may sound difficult, but the reverse is the case, and their use practically makes error impossible. The method is explained and exemplified in the ephemeris, and therefore requires no treatment here.

To insert Planets : Birth Abroad

The positions in the ephemeris are for noon at Greenwich, and therefore are only true as noon-positions for places using Greenwich time.

For all other places, the time in which birth is recorded (whether local or standard for the country) must be reduced to Greenwich. To do this, find the difference between Greenwich and the longitude of the place for which the recorded time is reckoned (place of birth if time is local, or, if time is standard, the meridian for which the standard time of that country is reckoned).[1] Then turn the difference into time at the rate of four minutes for each degree, adding this to the time if the birth-place is west and subtracting it if east. The result is the corresponding Greenwich time, for which calculate the planetary positions from the ephemeris in the ordinary way.

This method applies equally to places south of the equator.

As an example take a birth at noon at New York. This time would be recorded in U.S.A. "Eastern time" which is for 75° east. This equals 5 hours, and as it is west it must be added to the time to yield the Greenwich equivalent. Therefore, calculate the planets for 5 p.m.

Again, if birth were at Melbourne, Australia, at noon, we should have to subtract 10 hours and reckon the map for 2 a.m. Greenwich, because Melbourne uses a meridian of 150° east.

For many purposes it is sufficient to calculate planets and angles to the nearest degree or half-degree.

But if you do this do not insert the minutes ; put the nearest degree and omit them altogether. To insert them would imply that they have been calculated. Thus, 11.49 ♒ may be written as 12 ♒ ; 7.24 ♉ , as 7 ♉, or 7½ ♉.

In inserting the signs it is quite possible that you will be surprised to find some apparently absent. In these latitudes it often happens that one sign will cover one house completely and also the cusp of the next, so that it covers

---

[1] See table at end of this Chapter.

two cusps. Another sign will then be, so to speak, squeezed into a house without being either on its cusp or that of the next house. It is then termed *intercepted*, and should be written as shown in the cases of ♈ and ♎ in the example on page 42. At the equator or near it there are no interceptions, whereas in Scotland it is possible for two signs to be intercepted in the same house.

Example.—Required a horoscope for 2.44' p.m., January 1, 1924, at Sheffield.

We can for this purpose use Liverpool Houses, the difference in latitude being slight. The long. is about 1° 30' west.

	hrs.	min.	sec
S.T. Noon 1st January, 1924	18	39	30
Correction One			1
Time of birth p.m.	24	4	0
Correction Two			27
	21	23	58
Correction Three (subtract for west longitude)			6
	21	17	58

Turning to the tables of houses for Liverpool we find a S.T. of 21 hours 17' 49", which is very near, and is quite close enough for approximate work. We then copy out the degrees given in the table, making the asc. 26° ♊, for if it was 25° 30' at S.T. 21 hours 17' 49", then at 21 hours 17' 58" it must be a little more, and therefore nearer 26° ♊ than 25° ♊. We should enter the M.C. as 17° ♒, but not as 17° 0', because this would be incorrect. A little sum will show us that at 21 hrs. 17' 58" the ascendant is really 25° 32' ♊ and the M.C. 17° 2' ♒.

The cusps of the succeedent and cadent houses are always taken to the nearest degree only.

To calculate the planets, we take the Greenwich time (since Sheffield uses this standard) without any correction, i.e., 2 hrs. 44' p.m.

The log. for this time is 0.9435.

Add this to the log. for the daily motion of each planet, and the result is the log. of the motion of that body in 2 hrs. 44'. Since the birth was p.m. *add* this to the planets' noon-positions, and you obtain their places at birth.

Two examples should suffice :—

Daily motion of Moon to nearest minute =
14° 28' =	0.2198
Add log. of 2 hrs. 44' =	0.9435
	1.1633

This is seen to equal 1° 39'. Add this to the Moon's noon-position, which is 0° 58' ♏ and we have 2° 37' ♏ as the ☽'s position at birth.

Now take Mars :—

Daily motion of Mars between noon 1st January and noon 2nd January is 39' = log.   1.5673

Add log.   0.9435

$$2.5108 = 4'$$
(approximately)

4' is then added to the noon-position, yielding 18° 19' ♏.

It is easy roughly to check this result. 2 hrs. 44' is obviously somewhat less than one-eighth of the day of 24 hrs., therefore the result must be something less than one-eighth of 39', which it is in fact seen to be.

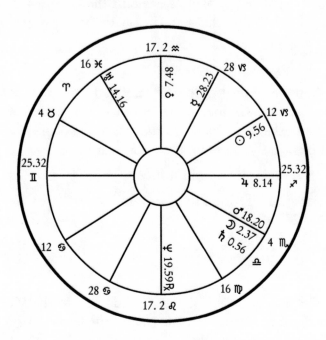

Jupiter, Saturn, Uranus and Neptune move so slowly that it will not be worth while to calculate their positions by the foregoing method. For example, the daily motion of Jupiter at the above time is seen to be 12'; an eighth of this would be 1½' and as 2 hrs. 44' is less than one-eighth, Jupiter's motion will be less than 1½', that is, it will be stated, to the nearest minute, as 1'. Saturn's motion is 4', so that, in an eighth of the day, it would be ½, and as our time is less than one-eighth we should make no alteration to the noon-position at all, because his motion will be nearer nothing than 1'.

We now have our horoscope complete, as shown opposite.

Further Considerations

Retrogression.—We have said that the planets' proper motion is in the order of the signs, that is to say, it is the reverse of that of the hands of the clock and is from west to east, whereas their apparent motion, due to the earth's rotation, is from east to west.

At times, however, they appear to slow down, remain stationary, and then reverse their proper motion. Then, after a while, they slow down again, remain stationary, and then resume their normal movement. The Sun and Moon are the only exceptions.

The reason for this is not hard to understand.

Imagine yourself walking in a circle round a central point, while another person does the same, in the same direction, but at a different distance, either greater or less than yours. A moment's reflection will show you that when he is on the same side of the centre as yourself he will seem to be going in one direction (if you watch him on the background of the various objects in the room, as we watch the planets on the background of the fixed stars), whilst when he is on the opposite side of the centre he will appear to be moving in the reverse direction.

Planets are therefore said to be *direct* when going in the sense of the zodiac, but *retrograde* (written ℞) when not doing so, and they can be *stationary to direct* or *stationary to retrograde.*

Retrograde motion is said to weaken planets, and to delay the fruits of their action, though it is debated whether these effects operate only in lessening and hindering benefic action, or whether evil action is also diminished, supposing they are in bad aspect.

A more modern view is, that retrograde planets tend to operate inwardly, for good or evil according to the aspects concerned. Hence, in a good map, retrogression may indicate a profound character, but in a mentally undeveloped type it may spoil material results without any compensating interior strength. It is suggested that direct motion and retrogression are in planets, what positivity and negativity are in signs.

Declinations.—These must be calculated from the ephemeris. The motion is so slow that the correct figures can usually be obtained in all cases (except that of the Moon) by mere inspection. The Moon can be worked in the same way as for longitude.

Tabulation of Aspects.—At first the beginner will find aspects difficult to detect, and he will probably attempt to find them by counting the signs intervening between the bodies, in which case he must beware of intercepted signs. Later he will learn to see aspects quite easily by observing the signs occupied by the bodies he is examining.

All signs of the same element are in trine, and all of the same quality in square. Fire and air signs are in sextile or opposition, and similarly water and earth.

The beginner may advantageously omit the minor aspects, viz. ⚹, ⚺, ∠, and ⊼.

THE ERECTION OF THE HOROSCOPE

The aspects in the horoscope on page 42 may be tabulated as follows :

	☽	☿	♀	♂	♃	♄	♅	♆	Asc.	M.C.	Declination
☉	✶					✶					23.5 S
☽		□	□				☌	⊥			4.46 N
☿			P		P	□	∠				20.49 S
♀					✶	□					20.0 S
♂							△	□		□	16.36 S
♃											21.0 S
♄							⊥	△			9.33 S
♅											6.54 S
♆									✶	☍	15.4 N

Note that in this form of tabulation each aspect is only entered once, and in order to see what aspect a body has it is necessary to go down the vertical line, headed by its symbol, until one reaches the horizontal line belonging to it, and then travel along that horizontal line. Thus, to find the aspects of Venus above, we begin with the vertical line, and see that it is □ ☽ and ☿; then we run along the horizontal line, and find that it is ✶ ♃ and □ ♄.

Observe that when bodies are in the same declination and also in aspect it is usual to enter the aspect and disregard the parallel, which in that case probably has no further effect than to strengthen the aspect according to its nature.

Students should cultivate care and neatness in drawing up horoscopes. Proper forms can be bought cheaply, while a loose-leaf ledger or card-index system will appeal to those who aim at a really useful collection of nativities. A rubber stamp, in the usual horoscopic form, can be bought from a stationer's for a few shillings, and forms can then be printed *ad lib.* on cards, pages of books, etc. as may be desired.

SUMMER TIME

The times of introduction and end of British Summer Time are as follows :

1916 2 a.m.	21st May to 3 a.m.	1st October
1917	8th April	17th September
1918	24th March	30th September
1919	30th March	29th September
1920	28th March	25th October
1921	3rd April	2nd October
1922	26th March	8th October
1923	22nd April	16th September
1924	13th April	21st September
1925	19th April	4th October
1926	18th April	3rd October
1927	10th April	2nd October
1928	22nd April	7th October
1929	21st April	6th October
1930	13th April	5th October
1931	19th April	4th October
1932	17th April	2nd October
1933	9th April	8th October
1934	22nd April	7th October
1935	14th April	6th October
1936	19th April	4th October
1937	18th April	3rd October

The Summer Time Act of 1922 laid down for subsequent years that " the period of Summer time shall be taken to be the period beginning at two o'clock Greenwich mean

TIME ZONES

Hours + or − of Greenwich	One Hour = 15⁰ of *Longitude* To find Corresponding G.M.T. *subtract* hours *plus* and *add* hours *minus*.
12 +	Fiji Islands
12 +	New Zealand
11 +	New Hebrides
10 +	Victoria, New South Wales, Queensland, Tasmania, New Guinea
9½ +	South Australia, Northern Territory of Australia, part N.S. Wales
9 +	Japan, Korea
8 +	Hong Kong, Philippine Islands, West Australia
7 20'+	Java
7 +	French Indo-China, Malay States, Straits Settlements
6½ +	Burma, Andaman Islands
5½ +	India, Ceylon
4 +	Mauritius
3 +	Madagascar, Russia, Iraq
2½ +	Kenya
2 + (East- European)	Turkey, Greece, Bulgaria, Roumania, Western Russia, Esthonia (except Reval), Latvia, Finland, Palestine, Egypt, Rhodesia, Union of South Africa, and Portuguese East Africa
1 + (Mid- European)	Germany, Lithuania, Sweden, Norway, Denmark, Austria, Poland, Hungary, Switzerland, Italy, Czecho-Slovakia, Yugo-Slavia, Nigeria, Sardinia, Sicily, Malta, Congo, Portuguese West Africa
19' 32" +	Holland (since May 1, 1909–prior to this date local time was used)
0+ (Greenwich time)	Great Britain and Ireland,[1] France, Belgium, Gibraltar, Spain, Portugal, Corsica, Algeria
1 −	Iceland, Madeira
3 −	Eastern Brazil
3½ −	Uruguay
4 − (Atlantic)	Canada (east of 67⁰), Nova Scotia, Barbadoes, Central Brazil, Argentine
4½ −	Venezuela
5 − (Eastern)	Canada (67⁰–89⁰), Eastern U.S.A., Jamaica, Cuba, Peru, Panama, Western Brazil
6 − (Central)	Central portions of Canada and U.S.A., Florida, part of Mexico
7 − (Mountain)	Canada west of 103⁰, Rocky Mountains States of U.S.A., Mexico
8 − (Pacific)	British Columbia and Pacific Coast States of U.S.A.
10 −	Alaska
10½ −	Hawaiian Islands
	NOTE: Most of these Zone Times were introduced in the various countries mentioned towards the end of the 19th century, prior to which they used the meridian of the respective capital cities.

[1] Since 21st May, 1910, prior to which Dublin time was used,
which is 0 hr. 25 21" slower than Greenwich.

time, in the morning of the day next following the third Saturday in April, or, if that day is Easter-day, the day next following the second Saturday in April, and ending at two o'clock, Greenwich mean time, in the morning of the day next following the third Saturday in September."

This act was renewed for 1924 and 1925 and was made permanent by an act of August, 1925, which lengthened the period by substituting the first Saturday in October for the third Saturday in September.

It is advisable to note the beginning and end of Summer time in your ephemerides year by year.

The New Russian Calendar

This was introduced under a decree taking effect from 1st January, 1930, and is instituted for the whole of the Soviet dominions.

The year consists of 72 weeks of 5 days each, Saturday and Sunday being abolished. There are 12 months, each containing 6 weeks.

Besides these 360 days there are 5 feast-days, which are:

1. Lenin's Day, which falls after the 30th January and before the 1st February.

2. The two Days of the Proletariat, which fall after 30th April.

3. The two Days of the Revolution, which fall after 30th October.

In leap-years a sixth feast-day (that of Industry) is to be inserted at a point not yet determined.

CHAPTER THREE

THE SUN, MOON, AND PLANETS
IN DETAIL

§ I. Planetary Strength

THE Sun, Moon, and Planets are all present in every horo-scope, and their action is to some extent felt in the life of everyone. But in this respect each nativity varies.

A planet may be strong or weak with regard to (*a*) sign-position, (*b*) house-position, and (*c*) aspects ; that is to say, *zodiacally, mundanely,* or by *aspect.*

It is strong mundanely if it is angular, and weakest if it is cadent. It is always stronger when near the cusp of a house than when it is near the end, so that the very stron-gest places are the cusps of angles, especially the asc. and the M.C. But mundane strength has relation to prominence in the life, or, on the other hand, to obscurity, rather than goodness or badness of influence. Mars exactly rising will be very prominent in the life of the native, for example, but whether it has a good effect or an evil depends rather on sign and aspect. Similarly a planet at the end of the 6th house is not likely to figure prominently in the life, but such action as it has will be good or ill according to sign and aspect.

Angular positions favour manifestation in action ; suc-ceedent work out largely through the feelings, and so may

49

be repressed for long periods ; cadent positions largely affect thought, and so may remain in the " subconscious " for years, although their influence is there all the time.

Zodiacal and aspectual strength decides whether the action of the planet will be harmonious and easy, or distorted, troublesome, and apt to lead one astray. A planet is strongest in its own signs, and, after that, in its exaltation, although it is thought by many that in the former case it is rendered more powerful, and in the latter actually manifests a finer and more desirable action. Thus it is often found that Saturn in Capricorn is simply a very clearly marked and decided Saturnian influence, whereas Saturn in Libra is refined and rendered less austere.

We will now consider the typical action of the various bodies, beginning with those ruling fire and water signs, and then passing to those that rule earth and air, and ending with Uranus, Neptune and Pluto, whose rulerships (if any) are uncertain.

§ 2. THE SUN ☉

The Sun is the ruler of Leo, fixed fire. From it come all the positive powers of our nature, all those that urge us outward and forward, and make for strong and vigorous manifestation on the physical plane. A well-placed Sun makes for dignity, self-reliance, strength of character, just appreciation of one's value, abundant affections, and ready helpfulness, with powers of leadership, control, and command. There are virile animal spirits, buoyancy, magnanimity, and a large and open way of viewing and dealing with life.

If the Sun is obscurely placed these qualities are lacking.

A prominent but afflicted Sun (i.e. strong mundanely, but weak by sign and aspect) gives a semblance of the solar virtues, but they tend to run to excess and lack balance and common sense to control them ; the native is apt to be ostentatious, bombastic, promising much and performing little, trying to lead, but often being, in fact, a puppet in the hands of favourites and sycophants. The affection may degenerate into sensuality, maudlin sentiment, or mere verbal affection, masking real selfishness. The self-confidence is either excessive or else hides inner cowardice and incompetence.

We get, in fact, many of the qualities that one associates with a bad monarch.

The action of the Sun is fortifying and vitalizing in whatever part of the map it is placed.

§ 3. THE MOON ☽

As the Sun is the only body that exclusively represents fire, so, with the possible exception of Neptune, the Moon alone rules only water. It is the ruler of Cancer, cardinal water, and is exalted in Taurus.

As the Sun stands for the positive self-expressive part of our nature, so the Moon stands for the feminine, indrawn, receptive, and imaginative side. It tends towards carefulness, prudence, timidity, shyness, and the secluded domestic life, although the lunar person is often shrewd and practical in business. It is maternal, affectionate, sympathetic,

51

impressionable, given to moods, easily roused emotionally, changeful, and yet tenacious and enduring in regard to its own activities, just as women, though reputedly changeable, are patient and enduring in those phases of life that are their special work, and are braver *passively* than men.

The lunar nature dwells much in the past and has a long memory. It is inclined to be clannish, prejudiced, and narrow in its sympathies, which are at first often limited to the home and family, but can expand so as to include wider and wider circles.

There is often morbid sensitiveness and self-consciousness.

The action of the Moon may be described as fluctuating, variable, absorbent, and receptive.

§ 4. MARS ♂

This planet rules Aries, cardinal fire, and Scorpio, fixed water, and it is exalted in Capricorn. It is in its own nature fiery and in many respects resembles the Sun. Its action, however, is more energizing and less stable ; it gives physical activity, enterprise, push, courage, and endurance, showing the more positive side through Aries and the more passive through Scorpio. It bestows nerve, muscular power, and the ability to " rough it ".

It is quick, decisive, restless, apt to do things single-handed, and " run the show ", believing that no one else can do as well. It may be quarrelsome, reckless, self-opinionated, and excessive in words, feelings, and actions. In bad cases it may even give cruelty and brutality, and if prominent there is seldom great refinement, the tendency being to get on with things and not beat about the bush with what appear to it as needless courtesies.

There is a great dislike of interference and a love of freedom and personal liberty, which, in the case of an evolved Martian, may produce a valiant and idealistic fighter on behalf of the weak ; this, indeed, is the highest type produced by Mars.

Its action is sudden, explosive, and disruptive.

§ 5. JUPITER ♃

Jupiter rules Sagittarius, mutable fire, and Pisces, mutable water. It is exalted in Cancer, in which sign it gains kindliness and gentleness, and expands the sympathies of the sign beyond the home-circle to which they are apt to be limited.

Being an entirely mutable planet, its action is largely on the mental plane, and it makes the philosopher, scientist, theologian, and speculative thinker of all kinds. It has also great power in the moral and material worlds, making the nature kind, generous, hopeful, and loyal, while the fortunes are improved, and the native who comes strongly under its ray is likely to be a success in business and in society. In some respects it resembles the Sun and Mars, though more mental, and under affliction it runs, like these bodies, to excess of energy, optimism, and self-indulgence. The faith becomes an unbounded belief in luck and a reckless disregard of consequences, so that, although seldom anyone's enemy but his own, the Jovian often ruins himself by pushing his luck too far, taking unreasonable hazards, gambling, and wasting time, money, and energy.

Jupiter has much to do with sports, hunting, athletics, and also with fondness for animals.

An obscure Jupiter may denote a mean, joyless, pessimistic nature.

The action of the planet, when well placed, is that of orderly and healthy growth or increase.

It will be seen that the three fire bodies closely resemble one another. They all make for exuberance of life and self-expression, inclining to the aggressive and self-assertive. Under affliction they may be noisy, loud, quarrelsome, or vain, according to the special features of each case. When their influence is lacking, the native tends to have no warmth of nature, and to be spiritless, without ideals or enthusiasms, timid, unsocial, or humdrum.

We now come to three bodies, each of which rules one earth and one air sign. They operate chiefly mentally, the airy side being more akin to abstract thought, and the earthy to that which is concrete and tangible.

§ 6. VENUS ♀

This planet rules Libra, cardinal air, and Taurus, fixed earth. It is exalted in Pisces, wherein its sympathies expand; it loses its ultra-refinement and tendency to dislike " soiling its hands " with the affairs of its less fortunate brethren.

Venus is the planet of harmony, or adaptation, the highest expression of which, emotionally, is love.[1] The Venusian love is understanding, idealistic, and universal, while that of Leo is usually warmer and more passional.

---

[1] Sexual love, or desire, is a ☉ ♂ activity ; from this point of view ♀ is rather the beloved.

Every work that requires collaboration, unification, co-operation, and the joining of hands for a common purpose is under the influence of this planet, which enables people to see common interests where Mars causes them to see points of difference.

When strong it gives a well-balanced, impartial, fair, placid disposition, refined, and devoted to the arts, fond of social pleasures, often lovable, but, of itself, unfitted for arduous or disagreeable work. It may be said that as Jupiter gives prosperity, so Venus gives happiness, by harmonizing the emotions.

A prominent but afflicted Venus gives laziness, dependence on others, carelessness, lack of enterprise and confidence, a parasitic attitude, day-dreaming, and unpracticality. The attractions bestowed by the planet may be used hypocritically to secure advantages.

A Venus obscurely placed in the horoscope is apt to denote the native to be boorish and uncultured.

The action of the planet is gentle and harmonious, but not very strong as regards things of the physical world.

§ 7. Mercury ☿

This planet rules Gemini, mutable air, and Virgo, mutable earth, and is said to be exalted in its own sign, Virgo. By some it is considered exalted in Aquarius, where it becomes steadied and humanized.

As in the case of Jupiter, its signs are both mutable, so that it is essentially intellectual. When prominent, it gives a quick, inquiring mind and ready expression with tongue and pen. There is a strong sense of logic, and a rapid comprehension of facts, often with a taste for detail rather than generalities. It may be a brilliant talker, and often possesses encyclopaedic knowledge. Note that it is not imaginative. Imagination is rather lunar and Neptunian. It is exact, matter-of-fact, and critical.

Under affliction, the mental powers are seldom lessened, but their expression may be vitiated by a tendency to untruthfulness, exaggeration, sarcasm, or ill-temper, according to the nature of the affliction. There may be a liking for hair-splitting or quibbling, too great immersion in detail, or even a criminal misapplication of the mental powers, such as in slander, libel, defalcation, or theft.

An obscure Mercury spoils the mental abilities, or at least prevents the native from expressing them easily.

The action of the planet is quick, volatile, and uncertain.

§ 8. Saturn ♄

This body rules Aquarius, fixed air, and Capricorn, cardinal earth. It is exalted in Libra, wherein it becomes gentler and more merciful, for of itself Saturn is the planet of strict justice that demands full payment for all that it bestows. It is the planet of the concrete and practical, and gives a vivid sense of material values and what are called hard facts. When strong it gives most of the virtues of what may be called the "self-help" type, such as patience, perseverance, hard work, thrift, concentration, solidity, and reliability.

It is the planet of limitation, and even when well placed in the horoscope the native who comes much under its ray is apt to be limited and circumscribed in his views and sympathies, conservative, cautious, and narrow.

When ill-placed as regards sign and aspect, but prominent by house, it is apt to show meanness, selfishness, a sense of great responsibilities, and a despondent, sad outlook. In this respect it may be contrasted with the three fiery planets and their typical optimism and faith — in God, luck, or themselves, according to their stage in moral evolution. The true Saturnian usually believes that nothing can be won without hard work, and he has both the virtues and the vices of this belief. It is the planet of real worth, as apart from show and make-believe, and gives to all things their permanent and lasting qualities. On the other hand, by limiting the outgoing activities of fire, it causes checks, delays, and disappointments, and so becomes the planet of fate, which sets definite bounds to our efforts.

Its action is slow, thorough, and inevitable.

§ 9. Uranus. ♅

This planet is said by some to rule Aquarius and by others is connected with Scorpio, but in the writer's opinion it is doubtful if it rules these or any other signs, although it has more affinity with them than with the others. It has the energy of fire, the emotional nature of water, and the intellect of air, and is perhaps least allied to earth.

It bestows originality, versatility, ability of many kinds, and good intellectual powers, so that it combines something of Mars and Mercury, but in pursuit of a chosen end it will manifest the virtues of Saturn as well, and display patience, organizing powers, and hard common sense. It is also in some respects like the Sun, for it tends to seek out positions of power and responsibility, and abhors limitation or restriction.

When rising it gives an unconventional but good-natured type, outspoken and rough-and-ready.

Under affliction it easily manifests extreme eccentricity and produces a gifted but useless crank, always at loggerheads with custom, irrespective of whether this is supported by common sense or not, so that it spends its time and energies fighting needless battles with convention and authority. It may also display moodiness, morbid sensitiveness, and a particularly explosive and at the same time unforgetting temper, with bitter resentments of fancied slights and injuries, in this respect recalling the worse side of Scorpio. It is, therefore, a dangerous influence ; and while it may bestow unique powers, it may also produce very undependable and even dangerous characters.

Nearly all persons with Uranus prominent have a peculiar nervous constitution.

Its weakness in a map shows lack of originality and independence.

It is connected with occult as distinct from negative or mediumistic characteristics, and is claimed as peculiarly the astrological planet.

The action of Uranus is sudden, unexpected, drastic, and as a rule resistless.

§ 10. NEPTUNE ♆

This planet, like Uranus, was discovered in modern times and has no recognized sign-rulership but experience connects it with Pisces.

As Uranus resembles in some respects the Sun, Mercury, Mars, and Saturn, so Neptune recalls several other

58

planets. It has a delicate musical and artistic sense and a spirituality that recall Venus, while its connection with drugs and poisons is reminiscent of Scorpio.

It commonly produces extreme sensitiveness, physical and emotional, and is not only prominent in the nativities of musicians, but also mediumistic persons, clairvoyants, spiritists, and others of similar schools of thought. It is utopian and bohemian, though less militantly unconventional than Uranus.

It tends, under affliction, to show that the native has impossibly high standards and ideals, with resultant dissatisfaction with himself and the world at large.

Its action is apt to be illusionary, deceptive, and prone to involve things which it influences in confusion, false appearances, and misunderstandings.

When very strong it may cause great spirituality and other-worldliness, or, in an ordinary map, much success, which, however, is often impermanent or more apparent than real.

The action of Neptune is insidious, subtle, and gradual.

§ 11. PLUTO (Symbol not yet determined) [♇]

This body was discovered in the early part of 1930 and neither its astronomical nor its astrological character has as yet been fully determined.

It is considered by some that its name indicates a connection with Scorpio, and it may even be claimed as ruler of that sign.

Preliminary observations, based on such data as are available, lead the present writer to consider that its action is such as to cause hidden and subterranean states (which are often generated originally by Neptune) to break forth or erupt, like earthquakes or volcanoes bringing about a climax in the life with much disturbance and upheaval, followed by calmer and more wholesome conditions. This may occur in mundane affairs and circumstances, or it may operate in the emotions ; but in either case it will be analogous to the above-mentioned geological phenomena.

It seems by its action to indicate the openings and endings of chapters in the life.

§ 12. Basic Psychological Concepts

The understanding of the planets will be easier after the student has obtained a clear idea of the meanings of the elements, as explained in the next chapter. We may, however, now tabulate some of the chief concepts connected with them :

	Good	Bad
The Sun	" Personality " Leadership Magnanimity	" Side," bluff, bombast. Favouritism
The Moon	Sympathy Protectiveness Prudence Love of home and country	Timidity Clannishness and prejudice Sentimentality
Mercury	Intellect Powers of expression	Dishonesty, lying, bad temper
Venus	Content Harmony Affection	Apathy Indolence, peace at any price Lack of moral stamina
Mars	Courage Energy	Quarrelsomeness, roughness Destructiveness Egotism

	Good	Bad
Jupiter	Hope	Over-optimism
	Generosity	Waste
	High Spirits	Horse-play
	Piety	
Saturn	Prudence	Lack of vision
	Self-control	Narrowness
	Practicality	Worldliness
Uranus	Originality	Perversity
	Genius	Eccentricity
	Force of character	Self-will
Neptune	Inspiration	Utopianism
	Spirituality	Worry
		Deception

The expression of the higher side of each planet is easy or difficult according to the general tenor of the nativity and the particular strength of the planet itself, especially (so far as character goes) with regard to the sign it occupies.

At the same time the student will not need to be told that no sensible person will seriously try to make planetary configurations a justification for moral failings. Bad positions do, to a certain extent, provide an excuse for our faults and render them understandable when they would not otherwise be, but, while they may make the attainment of a high moral standard difficult, they can never make it impossible ; and the astrologer, being one to whom much is given, is also one from whom much may legitimately be required. Many fine characters have much-afflicted maps.

Further, note that although the influences of the planets have been given above in terms of mind and character, it does not follow that they always work in that manner, as we shall see later. They are, however, essentially the same, upon whatever plane they operate.

CHAPTER FOUR

THE QUALITIES, ELEMENTS, AND SIGNS IN DETAIL

§ 1. THEIR MUTUAL RELATIONS

WE have enumerated the classes into which the signs are divided in Chapter One. A more careful study of these divisions is now requisite, for we may safely say that, from the psychological standpoint, if not from that of fate or destiny, the qualities and elements are of primary importance. Indeed, although they are but seven in number, the student who has got a clear conception of what they stand for will have gone a very long way towards understanding the astrology of character.

Reference should be made to the table on page 18.

Note that the four mutable signs are ruled by Mercury and Jupiter, which rule these and no others, so that they may be considered purely mutable in nature. On the other hand the Sun-Moon (which two bodies must for the purpose of psychological study be treated as the positive and negative aspects of one principle, as indeed they are), Venus, Mars, and Saturn each rule one cardinal and one fixed sign. Hence there is no such thing as exclusively cardinal or fixed planetary force.

Then, again, we have seen in the last chapter that the fire-water signs, on the one hand, and air-earth on the other,

62

are grouped apart by the fact that no planet rules one of each class.

To illustrate these points we may reproduce the table on page 18, substituting the planetary rulers in each case for the signs :

	FIRE	WATER	AIR	EARTH
Cardinal	Mars	Moon	Venus	Saturn
Fixed	Sun	Mars	Saturn	Venus
Mutable	Jupiter		Mercury	

§ 2. THE QUALITIES

These are also called the Quadruplicities, because each comprises four signs.

The *Cardinal Signs* stand for Activity, or Doing. They show free manifestation in the outer world, and produce energy, push, and enterprise.

Under affliction the cardinal signs show the restless and inconstant busybody, always beginning new projects and then forsaking them, without any settled policy, and given to interfering freely with others. Absence of this quality causes lack of initiative and lethargy.

The *Fixed Signs* are concerned chiefly with Feeling and the " pleasure-pain " aspect of things. Thus where a cardinal person would ask with regard to something fresh, " How will it affect what I want to do ? " the fixed person would ask " Is it pleasant or disagreeable ? "

The fixed sign persons are conservative, stable, set in their habits and opinions, strong in their likes and dislikes, and obstinate. They change seldom, but when they do their changes are often very drastic.

Under affliction they are lazy, self-indulgent, stubborn, bigoted, and stupid.

Lack of the quality shows absence of principle, ballast, and consistency.

The *Mutable Signs* are intermediate between the two other qualities, having something of each. They stand for Thought and the impartial mental attitude towards things, seeking to understand without bias. They are usually clever, mentally quick and alert, adaptable, changeful, and what is still called " mercurial ". They represent those who study and write about the actions of others, rather than themselves trying to " make history ".

We may mention in illustration some of the social types that come under these qualities.

Cardinal.—Leaders and men of action, pioneers, people with a goal and purpose in life.

Fixed.—The landowner and squire, and to a large extent the proprietors of old-established conservative businesses, as apart from the cardinal people who build them up. Most officials and people who " occupy positions ", especially those involving the exercise of authority and upholding of rules and regulations rather than finding out new ways and means.

Mutable.—All go-betweens, agents, and commissionmen ; students of all sorts ; inventors, writers, publishers, journalists ; those who describe and comment upon the doings of others, but are themselves impersonal ; philosophers and men of science, literature, and art.

It is to be observed that a quality or element is predominant or deficient according to the number of planets in signs of that nature, and in the word " planet " we include the ascendant. Planets themselves can also, by their prominence, make up for lack of an element or quality. Thus a person with Mercury rising would never lack the mutable quality, and one with the Sun rising would always possess a certain amount of fire, whatever else the map might contain. This point is important.

The qualities are not difficult to understand, despite their profound significance.

We now pass on to the elements or triplicities.

§ 3. THE ELEMENTS

The *Fiery Element* comprises Aries, Leo, and Sagittarius. Its function is self-assertion and active manifestation. It is positive, forceful, self-confident, and aggressive ; inclined to faith and optimism ; fond of good living, sport, exercise, company, and adventure ; always ready for what is new, and never afraid to face hazards and take the chances of life and circumstances.

The faults are such as spring from too robust, vigorous, and exuberant life, such as extravagance and all sorts of excess, recklessness, overhopefulness, pride, arrogance, coarse animal spirits, and lack of sympathy for the weak.

Without fire the native tends to lack enthusiasm, spirits, *joie de vivre*, and aliveness ; he becomes matter-of-fact, humdrum, and over-serious.

The *Water Signs* are Cancer, Scorpio, and Pisces. They are the opposite of fire, and show the shrinking, fearful, self-protective instinct, without which fire would cause life, whether in man or beast, to exhaust itself with sheer extravagance of vigour, or destroy itself through lack of prudence and excess of confidence.

The virtues of water are therefore prudence and foresight, sympathy and the desire to shield and protect, whilst its failings are such as arise from timidity, suspicion, fearfulness, or distrust of self and others. Scorpio, being ruled by Mars, shows the timidity least ; nevertheless, though physically courageous if put to the test, it inclines to suspiciousness and self-repression. All the water signs are sensitive and tend to keep themselves and their feelings to themselves, while fire is always self-expressive.

It will be seen that a horoscopic clash between fire and water denotes much inharmony, the two elements rending the native's nature asunder in the attempt to express on the one hand and repress on the other.

Fire and water are largely primitive and instinctive, having to do with our spontaneous emotions and impulses rather than with deliberately planned ideas. Earth and air are mental and purposive, the one being the executant, the other the designer.

Air is intellectual, refined, thoughtful, and devoted to the arts and sciences, especially from the more abstract and theoretical point of view. Its virtues lie in its idealism and desire for truth. It is co-operative, unitive, and harmonious in action, and is perhaps best seen in the domain of pure intellect. By itself it tends to become divorced from the real and practical, and to spend its time in day-dreaming ; it works with ideas rather than concrete objects, and, in the case of the less evolved, merely gives some artistic taste without either energy or ability to make use of it. When the practical part of the horoscope is also well developed there is considerable power for both planning and carrying out great works, and we get the practical engineer, designer, architect, and social and religious idealist.

Earth represents the brain applied to material ends, and is the craftsman, builder, and practical scientist. It may be said that civilization, in its material aspects, is chiefly the work of this element, which has raised us from the animal to the mastery of the physical world. The same lack of idealism and respect for the abstract and spiritual sides of life that we note in modern civilization is the fault of earth, when unredeemed by air. It becomes materialistic, sordid, commonplace, utilitarian in a narrow sense, and a slave to routine, law and order. It is a limiting element, and those who are largely composed, astrologically, of earth tend to be dry, matter-of-fact, and circumscribed in their outlook. On the other hand, lack of earth produces inability to bring forth tangible and useful results.

We pass now to a consideration of the signs.

§ 4. THE SIGNS IN DETAIL

We have seen on page 18 that the twelve signs are the outcome of dividing the zodiac into four elements and each element into three signs, one of each quality.

Observe that fire and water, being emotional, have much in common with the fixed quality, while air and earth, being mental, have much in common with the mutable. Hence a sign that belongs to an element congenial to its quality produces a very marked action of that nature. As, for example, Gemini, which is mutable-air, and therefore very intellectual in its manifestation, while Pisces, mutable-water, has no such similarity of element and quality, and produces consequently an unsettled temperament, the mind and feelings both being active and often at variance.

Double Signs

Gemini, Sagittarius, and Pisces are traditionally called " double ". They are characterized by much restlessness and lack of concentration and one-pointedness. Both in life and character they often show a curious doubleness. Thus there are often two separate vocations, either at the same time or consecutively, and frequently two marriages. These signs also tend to produce twins.

We shall now set forth in twelve short essays the leading characteristics of the signs. It is necessary to learn to blend these values with those of the planets that may occupy the signs, and, in the case of the signs being on the ascendant, to take into consideration the position of the ruler of that sign by house and sign, and its aspects. It will be seen that no text-book can deal with all possible combinations, but, by studying the principles involved, the student will be able to judge these as he meets them.

These essays are mainly written of the signs when on the ascendant, but a stronger and truer effect is usually seen when the Sun occupies a sign, and this is specially true of Cancer, Libra and Capricorn, which do not manifest well on the asc., because they correspond to the houses which are in square and opposition to it. The Sun is the basis of all horoscopes.

The sign-position and aspects of Mercury, modified by its aspects and house, will indicate the expressive powers of the native.

The other planets will produce effects according to their respective natures in whatever sign they may occupy.

ARIES ♈

This is a cardinal-fire sign, the positive sign of Mars and the exaltation of the Sun. It represents the crude outrush of manifesting life, and is characterized by extreme activity, especially physical. There is unlimited energy, daring, love of enterprise and adventure, and a quick, decided temper that ill brooks any opposition or restraint. In good types the courage and vigour are devoted to sensible and useful ends, and the native may achieve much as a reformer or advocate of the weak. In bad types the native is quarrelsome, " spoils for a fight ", will not compromise, and sees only his own point of view. The daring becomes foolhardiness, and there is an entire lack of common prudence and foresight. There are disastrous outbreaks of temper and feats of empty bravado, and the native is liable to be victimized by anyone who cares to arouse him by taunts or provocative challenges. Aries rarely looks before it leaps, and there are few natives of the sign who do not, at some time or another, do foolish and short-sighted things. The mind is often quick and able in dealing with concrete things, but it is essentially a sign of action, ignores theoretical considerations, and it likes to rely on the inspiration of the moment to see things through. It is a good advocate, but a poor judge, for it finds impartiality difficult.

TAURUS ♉

The negative sign of Venus and exaltation of the Moon. Fixed-earth.

This is in most respects the opposite of Aries. It is slow, careful, steady, practical, and reserved. It tends to inertia, and is often lazy, sensuous, and selfish. It is easily contented, and enjoys the simple things of life, especially those of a rural nature. It is motherly, homely, and protective. In business it is conservative, and likes safe and well tried methods. In good types there is much patience, perseverance, firmness, and determination, but these are often negative and passive virtues, and the native will do little without definite stimulus. It makes a good administrator, and can keep order and discipline easily. There is usually a high sense of probity, especially in all matters concerning money. The temper is peaceable and not easily roused, but when once provoked Taurus can be violent and unrelenting.

There is a good sense of colour and of tune, and the sign produces many fine singers. Otherwise the sign tends to agricultural pursuits, and seems commoner and truer to type in the country than in towns.

GEMINI ♊

Gemini is an airy or intellectual sign, and is ruled by Mercury.

It is pre-eminently the sign connected with the concrete mind, or that part of the mind which deals with facts and figures rather than with ideals and experiments. It is the sign of reason and logic, and Geminians excel all others in their ability to grasp conceptions clearly and logically. Hazy or sentimental thinking, leading to loose or inaccurate conclusions, are particularly distasteful to them, and, while able to deal with abstractions, and usually very interested in literature and art, they are always capable of examining things from the rational standpoint without any emotional bias. They are more matter-of-fact than sentimental, and admire and like brain and cleverness. They are nearly always mentally active themselves and are quick at repartee, being bright and energetic conversationalists, good debaters, and keen at argument. There is much mental vivacity and agility.

The faults of the sign are lack of concentration and the tendency to take on too many projects and enterprises, so that they have " too many irons in the fire ", and leave things unfinished. Only when this diffusive tendency is overcome can the sign get the most from its fine intellectual powers. There is lack of decision and a good deal of wavering and difficulty in making up the mind. The Geminian often excels in detail, and may lose himself in it, failing to " see the wood on account of the trees ". Emotionally there is a distinct tendency to egoism, hardness, and selfishness, Gemini people being too mental to develop warmth of heart. Even when the rest of the nativity shows generosity of feeling, it cannot manifest freely and easily through Gemini. There is often too great a liking for introspection, with resultant self-centredness and discontent. There is sometimes flippancy and irreverence.

Under severe afflictions there may be deceit, untruthfulness, or dishonesty.

Physically Gemini is very active, the limbs, eyes, and expression being in constant change. They are restless and changeful, seldom settling down. In many respects they resemble children and retain their youth for long. They often dislike old people, but at the same time, are not fond of young children, and make bad mothers or nurses, owing to their highly strung nervous system.

They come much into contact with books and writings, and make excellent clerks, teachers, and students. Their happiest days are often those spent at school and college, where they easily hold their own.

CANCER ♋

This is a cardinal water sign, ruled by the Moon.

Cancerians are noted for their extreme sensitiveness, both physical and emotional. They are commonly very moody, and at the same time, owing to their cardinal quality, their moods vary rapidly, usually reflecting each outside influence with which they come into contact. This is particularly true of ♋ *rising*; the Sun in ♋ has a steadying effect. The primitive type is imaginative, emotional, and sentimental, while its sensitiveness renders it extremely timid and even helpless. There may be morbidity and sensationalism. The advanced type shows the same sensitiveness, but has control of its feelings, and, while retaining deep and ready sympathies, is more judicious and discriminating in expressing them.

In primitive types of all the water signs there is danger of moral weakness, owing to the activity of the sensational nature and the ease with which impressions of all sorts are absorbed. Cancer is, however, to a certain extent paradoxical. It is the sign of the " Eternal feminine ", and, just as women are in one aspect very weak, and in the other very courageous and able to endure pain and suffering that the more positive male could not undergo, so Cancerians may show much tenacity and passive bravery, especially when the maternal or protective side of the nature is roused. They have the greatest sticking power of the signs, and once they have taken up a position or idea they maintain it with a persistence which is not found in more objective signs.

They are usually good business people, being shrewd, thrifty, prudent, and careful. They proceed cautiously and often almost imperceptibly, without much noise or self-advertisement, except in so far as business may require.

The domestic side is usually strong ; they are home-loving and devoted to their families. Often there is much clannishness, prejudice against strangers, and a tendency to make the family the end of their existences. The love of the past and of old things is strong ; the memory is retentive, and thoughts hark back readily to the past, in which they often live, while regarding the future very frequently with anxiety and misgiving.

LEO ♌

The sign Leo is of the fixed quality, and belongs to the fire element, being ruled by the Sun.

73

It is probably the sign of the Zodiac which possesses the greatest amount of *power*, using that word in the widest sense. Physically there is usually great vitality, and the same characteristic applies equally to the mental and emotional natures. There is usually some degree of ambition and a firm will, with considerable persistence, and, since these are usually united to a naturally effective personality, we seldom find the native of Leo occupying an obscure position. The inherent ability of the sign brings it forward and upward until it has achieved a position of prominence and authority, even though the native may not have any special talent. If, however, the nativity also shows real mental acuteness and judgment the native will go far. Few " born leaders " are without a strong solar influence, either through the Sun itself, or its sign, or both. Leo never likes to work in corners ; its destiny is to come to the front, deal with large issues, and leave drudgery and detail to others. It possesses all the gifts of the born commander, and produces people whom others readily respect and obey. Usually genial and often democratic in theory, its methods are nearly always autocratic. The tendency to delegate work is very strong in nearly all Leos, but in good types the Leo himself always remains, not a mere figure-head, but a real director and inspirer. Naturally in weak types this characteristic is easily perverted, and we get the kind of person who tries to win praise for himself from what has been done by humbler members of the zodiacal fellowship working under him.

The Leonian is temperamentally good-natured, obliging, and often even devotedly affectionate, but an element of patronage often creeps into his attitude towards others.

While making a good and open-handed master, there is often little inclination to regard others as equals, so that independent natures often find the sign irritating in its attitude towards them. On the other hand, weak and clinging natures find it a tower of help and strength, ever ready to pour out life, courage, and confidence from its own abundant stores.

The faults of the sign are those common to weak natures highly placed. They develop vanity, are easily flattered, surround themselves with favourites, aim at show rather than merit, and become assuming, snobbish, and worldly, promising much and achieving little. There is secret meanness beneath an appearance of pompous self-satisfaction.

Virgo ♍

This is the negative sign of Mercury, and is mutable-earth.

Its keynote may be said to be practical mentality, or the brain applied to concrete matters. Although usually artistic and literary, and gifted with considerable taste, Virginians seldom lack appreciation of the facts of life ; they are generally careful in money-matters, and possess sound commercial instinct. They are neat, methodical, precise, and without regard for show or pretentiousness, preferring to judge and be judged by results. They take a pride in their work, if it is at all congenial to them, and as a rule like to be left alone to carry out their tasks in peace and quiet. The abilities are very great for all work requiring good mental powers, conscientiousness, and attention to detail; they make excellent secretaries, or subordinates of any kind, but do not often assume control, dislike responsibility on a large scale, and shrink from the limelight and self-advertisement; in fact, they are often shy and retiring, making few friends, and often being particular about whom they meet socially.

They usually possess skill in manual craftsmanship, and either for a livelihood or a hobby cultivate such things as carving, metal-work, clock-making, or engineering. They are also often literary and possess unusual humour and whimsicality. Gardening also generally attracts them, and another characteristic is the marked interest in matters pertaining to health, diet, and hygiene. They are often doctors or physical culturists, and at times degenerate into valetudinarians.

Virgo is pre-eminently a sign of criticism and discrimination, especially as regards details, and the commonest failings of the sign are the outcome of this tendency. They may be chronic fault-finders, cantankerous, prejudiced, and narrow in their views, with the result that they are unpopular with those who misunderstand their natures. The love of method also leads to fussiness and immersion in detail, and their refinement may develop into prudery and lack of charity towards the lapses of warmer-blooded signs. At the same time many natives of Virgo are notably kind and ready to oblige those whom they recognize as friends.

LIBRA ♎

This is the positive sign of Venus and the exaltation of Saturn, and is cardinal air.

The outstanding characteristics are love of harmony,

justice, and sympathy for pain and suffering. There is a highly developed sense of beauty. The Librans are very social and companionable ; they seldom lead separative lives, and are always found doing their best work and achieving most happiness when associated with others, either in marriage or in some other form of partnership, such as a close friendship. They are affable, courteous, obliging, and very rarely guilty of a desire to injure others.

At the same time they are not fond of rough, ugly, or dirty conditions, and do not care to expose themselves to the more sordid aspects of life, so that they are ill-fitted for work that involves unpleasant associations, and are accused of being shallow and insincere.

The temper is even and equable, and if ruffled subsides readily. They never bear malice ; in fact, the memory is inclined to be short, and there is a readiness on all occasions to forgive and forget. They find a disturbed or quarrelsome atmosphere very hard to support, and give way or compromise rather than face prolonged discord.

In evolved types there is much sweetness and spirituality ; it is said that Libra alone of the signs can " touch pitch and not be defiled " ; even the most primitive types can generally respond to better things when an opportunity is given, and in many cases there is a marked longing for escape from worldly conditions, and a good deal of secret unhappiness in the face of the roughness and hardship of life.

They are rarely extreme in their views and are impartial ; and on this account they are valuable as go-betweens, emissaries of peace, and agents of all sorts, always working for harmony and the establishment of harmonious relationships.

The liking for the opposite sex is usually noticeable.

The faults are those of weakness and compliancy. They find it hard to say " No," or to take a firm attitude in the face of hostility, and tend to avoid unpleasantness at all costs. Hence they often compromise too much, "sit on the fence", and waver from one view to another without giving a downright reply which would commit them to one course. They are often lazy, and, while high types dress tastefully and well, the primitive ones may be slovenly and careless. They cannot act on their own responsibility, but instinctively seek a partner. There may be effeminacy, affectation (such as drawling), and they may be " spoilt children " or " milk-and-water " characters.

It is to be noted that the *Sun in Libra* differs widely from Libra rising and is far more energetic, sometimes noticeably so. It is also a position of disputatiousness and even of warfare, being common in the horoscopes of generals, public debaters, and propagandists ; it is often as loth to give way as Libra rising is prone to do so.

Scorpio ♏

The negative sign of Mars, and that of fixed water.

There is an intense emotional nature. No sign has more profound and enduring feelings, for owing to the fixity of Scorpio these become set, with the result that in high types there is unwavering devotion to ideals, deep sympathy, and true understanding, while in primitives, in whom the moral standard is low or uncertain, a host of dangerous feelings may appear — bitter dislikes or hatreds, often cherished for a lifetime, extreme sensitiveness to imagined slights or injustice, resentment, suspicion, and furious anger. Scorpios of this kind are very prone to think themselves under-valued, and to relieve their feelings on this score in the shape of constant boasting. There may be treachery, cruelty, and revengefulness. Sometimes these worse traits appear in childhood, but die out with good training. There are nearly always strong affections, and great care should be taken in training a Scorpio child that these are not ruined either by over-indulgence on the one hand, or harshness on the other. The physical endurance is very great, but the emotional nature needs the most careful treatment.

The sign is extremely thorough-going, and few flabby characters are born under it. There is usually much courage, and also great energy and capacity for toil in the pursuit of any aim which claims the native's devotion. As a result many heroes have been born under the sign, as well as many notable villains. They do nothing by halves, and, having once selected their course in life, pursue it relentlessly.

In primitives there may be reckless self-indulgence and in evolved ones intense devotion. The powerful feelings constantly tempt the native, and few Scorpios pass through life without having run the full gamut of temptation on the physical plane. Self-control and self-denial are the chief virtues that they need to develop.

The better types are noticeably dignified and endowed

with self-respect and proper pride ; they are often grave and restrained in their speech and demeanour, and do not readily unbend, even in society.

It is a sign that very frequently gives an inclination towards some form of mysticism or occultism, and it is prominent in most enthusiastic free-masons. There is a natural tendency towards what is secret and hidden, and a love of probing mysteries and getting at the bottom of things.

They excel as detectives, inspectors, and investigators of all kinds, make good surgeons and chemists, and frequently enter the Army or Navy.

SAGITTARIUS ♐

This a mutable-fire sign, and is ruled by Jupiter.

The typical Sagittarians are high-spirited, kind, generous, and honest, with a great love of outdoor life, sports, and athletics. They enjoy life to the full, and are always ready for convivial amusements of all sorts. The mental abilities are also as a rule above the average, and in good types there may be great interest in philosophy, metaphysics, and religion. There is a love of travelling, exploring, and wandering, and the sense of home is usually small.

Freedom and personal liberty make a strong appeal, but at the same time most Sagittarians also understand the need of law and order, and have no inclination towards violence in any form.

The faults of the sign are the result of its exuberance of life and spirits, and its restlessness and love of covering large stretches of country, both physically and mentally. There may be extravagance, carelessness over detail, waste, reck-lessness, too great faith in luck, superficiality, a tendency to know a little of everything but all of nothing, with sudden crazes for people, intellectual interests, and hobbies, which blaze up and die away, and also a certain degree of loudness and vulgarity.

It is, however, on the whole, one of the most fortunate and likeable of the signs, and even primitive examples are seldom anyone's enemy but their own.

CAPRICORN ♑

This is the negative sign of Saturn and the exaltation of Mars.

The Sun in Capricorn tends to produce a good Saturn type, careful, prudent, conscientious, ambitious, but just to others, justice being sometimes more pronounced than mercy. It is usually gifted, and, if it finds its right work, it may go far, especially in politics, commerce, and adminis-tration.

The failings which may occur in weak examples are such as worldliness, snobbishness, a tendency to manage and even to make use of others for private ends, narrowness of outlook, too great respect for the past and a refusal to change with the times and to progress. There may be down-right selfishness and craftiness in pursuit of personal advan-tage. The general abilities are usually good but are com-monly limited to so-called practical things.

Capricorn rising seems to give a much more emotional type, a love of music being a common characteristic. The conscientiousness and practical abilities are often less, so that this position will often produce clever but ineffective people, who seem unable to find their right place in the world and in consequence fret and flit capriciously from one thing to another, achieving little and often becoming sour and disappointed. It is a restless and sometimes rather self-important position and many examples are loquacious and pushing, disliking to be overlooked. It would seem that the Sun-Capricorn type is as a rule much more successful but has the limitations of its virtues, and it is probably correct to say that it is more often trusted and respected than loved.

It is often successful in scientific work, whereas Capricorn rising tends rather to the arts.

A strong Venus will do much to supplement the failings of this type, and this is indicated by the fact that the ruler is exalted in the refined and mild sign Libra.

AQUARIUS ♒

This is the positive sign of Saturn, by some held to be ruled by Uranus. It is fixed air.

It produces several rather distinct types. The purely Saturnian Aquarian resembles the Capricornian in his seriousness and his grave outlook on life, but he is as a rule far less practical ; the mind is much more idealistic, and may spend much time in abstract thoughts and dreams, often on problems of philosophy, religion, and sociology, and the result may be a lack of practical common sense. On the other hand, there is nearly always kindness, sympathy, and refinement, together with an intense love for and feeling of kinship with wild nature. There is generally artistic ability. The native tends to be attracted to societies, clubs, associations, groups of people, and " movements " of all sorts, easily merging his own personality in " causes ". There are many associates, but the temperament is often too detached to make warm friendships.

Aquarius has a great love of personal freedom, and resents enforced obedience, but apart from this it is usually faithful, constant, and affectionate. But, above all, it is the sign of truth and sincerity, and will not act a conventional lie, and it is this trait which sometimes leads it in direct opposition to ordinary ideas of morality, and may get it a reputation for looseness among those who are attached to the form rather than the reality. Uranus resembles Aquarius in this lack of conventional bias, but it is far fiercer and more uncontrolled in its hatred of restraint, having a Martian resentment and energy that seem foreign to the friendly and sympathetic Aquarian.

It is pre-eminently the human sign, and the very fact that it signifies mankind in general makes it hard to specify particular characteristics.

It should be recollected that in these latitudes nearly all persons with Aquarian ascendants have Pisces intercepted in the 1st house, and if there is a planet in that sign and none in Aquarius, both appearance and character will be largely Piscean.

PISCES ♓

The negative sign of Jupiter, with strong affinity to Neptune, and the exaltation of Venus.

Pisces is the most negative and plastic of the signs, and

it seldom possesses a very strong individual character, for it lives largely on the thoughts and feelings of those with whom it comes into contact. Hence it is, above all, the actor's sign, giving great ability to absorb and express the emotions of others. The imagination is extremely active, as in all watery signs, and the life is often passed in the imaginative rather than the actual world. Hence the sign is frequently prominent in the nativities of writers, poets, and artists.

The religious nature is often highly developed. The sympathies are very abundant, and the sign is attracted to the needy and sick and all those who require help. It may cause the native to connect himself with hospitals, asylums, or other refugees and institutions of a like description, as well as prisons, monasteries, and other places of a solitary nature.

In some types the desire to help others seems to find expression in the giving of advice and the preaching of "sermons" in and out of season.

There is usually much affection for animals and great love of the sea.

Pisceans are commonly jovial and convivial, and often make entertaining companions. They vary from the highest to the lowest spirits in incredibly short periods, and are equally ready to help others and themselves to apply for assistance, being often without much sense of responsibility, thriftless, and devoid of the most ordinary worldly wisdom. Indeed, a large proportion of life's wastrels are born under this sign, while it has undoubtedly produced some of the most spiritual characters of history. They are as a rule their own worst enemies, and, though not often violent or cruel, Pisces is capable of deceiving both itself and others, and produces bad examples of hypocrisy, especially of the religious kind.

Drugs have a great fascination for many Pisceans, who seem often to crave emotional and physical stimulation, but their physique is frequently by no means strong and indulgence in this direction generally produces rapid collapse. It is therefore, above all, necessary that they should carefully avoid the formation of habits of this character.

In the same way there is often a great love of various forms of spiritism, psychism, and cognate practices, which minister to the love of sensation, but often prove sources of danger.

CHAPTER FIVE

THE HOUSES IN DETAIL

§ 1

THE Houses are divisions of the visible heavens, as seen at any point of time at any place on the earth, with a corresponding division of the invisible heavens, hidden beneath the earth.

Every department of human life falls under one or other of the Twelve Houses. They are channels, so to speak, through which man enters into relationship with his environment. They have more distinct reference to physical things than the planets and signs, which are connected rather with the character and disposition. Yet mind, emotions, body, and circumstances act and re-act continuously and we cannot say definitely that any factor of the horoscope is *exclusively* related to one of these only.

Thus it is commonly said that the Sun, Moon, and planets may be taken to correspond to Spirit, the Signs to the Soul, and the Houses to the Body. But, whilst this may be true in an analogical sense, it will not be found very helpful in practical astrology. Some house-positions, for example, affect the character very markedly, as, for instance, a rising planet or a planet in the 3rd, and bodies in signs often have a quite material effect.

The correspondence between the Houses and the Signs is very easily traced.

THE HOUSES IN DETAIL

THE FIRST HOUSE

This rules the physical body, considered as the instrument through which the higher principles that make up man manifest materially. It affects health, temperament, and the physical build and appearance.

Everything that is in the horoscope has to manifest in everyday life *via* the rising sign, or sign on the cusp of the 1st house, which thus becomes a kind of lens through which all influences have to pass, suffering modification in doing so. Thus the 1st affects the more obvious and easily noticed part of the disposition ; it shows the person as he or she appears to the casual acquaintance, and denotes the *manners* of the individual, as much as any one part of the nativity may be said to do so.

THE SECOND HOUSE

This rules possessions of all kinds ; the material that goes to the support of the living body shown by the 1st, the financial condition and the native's attitude towards money, and his worldly resources.

It has some influence on his *feelings*, and what may be called true character, or principle, and must be taken into consideration in judging these things, especially if planets are in it.

THE THIRD HOUSE

This concerns relations and relationships and all means of intercommunication (upon which, of course, relationships depend, since one cannot be related to a thing without

87

a means of maintaining communications with it). Thus we have blood-relations,[1] especially brothers and sisters ; letters, books, and writing of all sorts ; short journeys (those that are of a routine rather than an explorative kind) ; all things that are used for such journeys, as trams, bicycles, and motors ; and, above all, speech, with which we are able to bring our own mind into contact with those of others.

Education also comes under this house, and the Mind generally is much influenced by it, as we shall see in Chapter Six.

The Fourth House

Like all three watery houses (i.e. 4th, 8th, and 12th, which correspond to the watery signs), this has a deep occult signification. It denotes both the beginning and the end of life, the womb and the grave ; it stands for all that is indrawn and secluded, and thus acquires as one of its commonest meanings that of the Home or the Private Life, and so it governs houses, land, and the early life at home. It is connected with the parents, and, paradoxically, is said to denote the father, although it corresponds to Cancer, ruled by the Moon.

It is questionable whether any house shows the parents of the native very clearly, but since both the vocation, public life, and status on the one hand, and the home-life on the other, depend largely on them, the meridian line (which is the cusps of the 4th and 10th) reflects to a considerable

---

[1]But in judging relations considerable attention must be paid to psychological actualities. For example, in so far as a person (whether related or otherwise) is an object of affection, the 5th house should be considered.

extent the dispositions and fortunes of the parents. Other factors affecting the parents will be explained in Chapter Seven, § 5.

This house is connected with mediumship, and if many planets are therein there is a sense of nearness to the " other side " of things that may or may not be beneficial to the native, according to the planets in the house and its ruler.

THE FIFTH HOUSE

Joys, pleasures, holidays, courtship, and all sorts of enterprises and new undertakings come under this house, as well as speculation and games of hazard ; also the birth of children and the native's own children. It is the house that corresponds to Leo, and through it the great creative and joy-engendering activities of the Sun find expression.

It denotes all objects of the native's *instinctive* affections, and thus is often indicative of the parents, brethren, playmates, pets, and sweethearts. Seriously afflicted, it may denote immorality, self-indulgence, profligacy, and all kinds of looseness due to desire for pleasure.

THE SIXTH HOUSE

In contradistinction to the 5th this is the house of work and toil of all sorts, by which the pleasures of the 5th are fed, just as the 2nd house feeds the Arietic forces of the 1st. It governs subordinates, servants of all kinds, and service. Hence, in so far as we subordinate ourselves to anything, whether it is an ideal or a person, we identify our activities with this house.

It is called the house of health, but the bodily well-being cannot, as will be explained, be judged solely from it.

THE SEVENTH HOUSE

Under this comes the principle of *partnership* in all its manifestations. Generally its influence is good, and it shows the husband or wife, the business partner, if any, and bosom-friends. Under affliction it may, however, assume a hostile significance, and show open enemies. It is the *other party* to all our bargains and in all negotiations.

It shows our ideal self, what we *would* be in contradistinction to the 1st house, which shows what we *are*, and it signifies what is complementary to and lacking in ourselves, and therefore is required by us in a partner to render us complete, and is dangerous to us in an enemy, because we lack it ourselves.

THE EIGHTH HOUSE

Traditionally the house of death. It shows the interplay of decay and regeneration, both physical and moral, the death of the old and the birth of new things from the ruins. It has significance in relation to health and accidents, and probably rules the effects that others have on one's health, as by infection and suggestion.

In the nativities of immoral and criminal types, this house, if heavily afflicted planets are in it, may show crime and retribution ; in the maps of ordinary worldly people it shows the property of the partner and money owed to the native, or his money in the hands of others.

It rules the goods of the dead, legacies, and settlements, and all occupations that have to do with death, such as undertaking and the meat trade.

It is the house through which the native is most closely related to the " astral plane " and the occult or cryptic forces operating on and from it ; and from the condition of the house may be deduced the sort of effects which the native will experience from this quarter, and the wisdom or otherwise of any endeavour on his part to communicate with its denizens.

THE NINTH HOUSE

This rules travel and exploration — long journeys into unknown places ; also *mental* exploration, as in metaphysical and philosophic thinking and speculative thought of all sorts. It rules foreign countries, the churches, and the law, as well as persons and things related to them.

It has much to do with inspiration and man's relation with spiritual things and beings. It is said to be connected with prophecy and with dreams.

It has much to do with man's moral nature and conscience.

THE TENTH HOUSE

This is the house wherein the physical and mundane activities of the native reach their pinnacle. It indicates the native's place in society, his standing before the world, and so, in part, his sense of honour, his ambitions, and his vocation, which last is frequently the result of his ambition and is the determinant, to a great extent, of his social status.

It is said to denote the Mother, but this is often questioned, see in this connection what is said above under the 4th house.

THE ELEVENTH HOUSE

This rules the hopes and aspirations, the joys of the spiritual part of the native, as the 5th stands for his pleasures on the lower side.

It shows the friends of the native and his associations with others in clubs, societies, and so forth.

It denotes his *spiritual and intellectual* ambitions or ideals.

THE TWELFTH HOUSE

This signifies sorrows, confinement, secret enemies, betrayals, and ambushes. Its sorrows are mainly caused by others, or affect others directly and the native indirectly because of his associations with the sufferers. In material things it is a house of limitation and loss, unless strongly tenanted, but in a spiritual sense it is indicative of self-sacrifice and the forsaking of worldly things for the life of the Spirit.

Strong planets in this house usually give eventual success, as they are carried towards the meridian by direction (see Chapter Ten), but the beginnings of life are often humble.

As the sixth house from the Seventh, the Twelfth is specially concerned with the health of the partner. It may also denote the native's illnesses, insofar as they cause confinement (especially in homes, hospitals, and similar institutions). The illnesses of this house are usually longer than those of the Sixth.

THE HOUSES IN DETAIL

It is worthy of observation that the last six houses tend to operate on a wider and more general scale than the first six. Thus, 1st house = the personal self, 7th = the public ; the 2nd = one's own property, the 8th = money of others associated with the native ; 3rd = short journeys of a routine character, 9th = long and explorative journeys ; 4th = home, 10th = vocation and standing ; 5th = pleasures (always limited), 11th = ideals (infinite) ; 6th = personal health, 12th = sorrows through others. The last six nearly always *involve other people.*

Houses are in all cases judged :

(a) By their *essential rulers,* or those bodies which rule the corresponding sign.
(b) By their *accidental rulers,* or those bodies ruling the sign on the cusp or intercepted.
(c) By their *occupants,* or the planets placed in them, if any.

The essential rulers commonly denote the native's attitude of mind towards the matter ruled by the house in question, while (*b*) and (*c*) denote the circumstances that arise out of it in his particular case.

Attention must be paid to the other house ruled by the accidental ruler ; such community of rulership connects the two houses and the matters they signify. Thus, in nearly all Libran horoscopes Mars rules the 2nd and the 7th, and thereby shows that the partner will affect the financial conditions more than is ordinarily the case. If Mars were in the 5th, this would be through the matters of this house, and so on. Judge from the strength of Mars how this connection would work out.

Again, consider the house ruled by a planet occupying the house under consideration, if there be any. For example, if the 10th house contains the lord of the 6th, and it is much afflicted, judge that the vocation will be affected adversely by health-troubles, bad servants, and so forth.

A conjunction of two planets also unites the affairs of the houses ruled, and, of course, any aspect brings them into mutual relationship according to their nature and that of the aspect. Thus, a planet in the 2nd trine one in the 5th shows gain through speculation ; a square, the reverse. These influences are, of course, far from simple, and much experience is needed before one can judge surely ; yet, if the student follows astrological teaching, it will not betray his confidence, intricate and even far-fetched as many of these rules must seem at first sight.

§ 2. SECONDARY HOUSE INFLUENCES

It is not customary to subdivide the houses into decanates and so on, but one class of sub-influence is of importance.

This arises when considering the affairs of people related to the native, as, for example, the financial affairs of the father. In order to arrive at the correct house we consider the house denoting the relative as his 1st house, and then count from that. Thus the father's money is the 2nd from the 4th, i.e., the 5th, and so on. Again, to judge the wife's health, do not merely consider the 7th, but look at the 12th and 2nd = her 6th and 8th. It is frequently to be noticed how a planet on the cusp of the 2nd influences the partner's health.

It is doubtful, however if the affairs of others can be detected in this way unless the native is to some degree affected by them.

§ 3. HOUSE-ORBS

It is generally considered that an orb of about 5° should be allowed beyond the cusp of each house, and a little more for angles. Some writers advocate extending this to as much as one-third of the preceding house, so that a planet in the last third of a house is considered in the next.

A simpler view seems to be that the houses as such have no orbs, but, as we have seen, the planets have, and thus, if a planet be within 8° or so of a house-cusp it is only natural that its effects will be felt partly through that house, as well as the house it is actually in.

Such positions often seem to link together the two houses in question in a way indicated by the planet. Thus, Mars in the 9th, but near the M.C., might show some loss (♂) of reputation (M.C.) through legal matters (9th).

§ 4. METHODS OF HOUSE DIVISION

Several of these have been advocated by different mathematicians, but the Semi-Arc method, used in Raphael's Tables, is at present almost universally employed.

This method was introduced by the mathematician *Placidus*.

Another system, first used by *Campanus*, a geometrician not to be confused with Campanus or Campanella, the Renaissance scholar and astrologer, is preferred by some on mathematical and logical grounds.

The third principal system is that of *Regiomontanus*, which was extensively used during the Middle Ages and later. It was ousted by the Placidian system but has recently regained ground on the Continent.

The method of *Porphyry* seems inconsistent.

According to some, the cusps of the houses should be regarded as the centres, rather than the beginnings, of the houses.

As tables for systems other than the Placidian are not at present easily obtainable in Great Britain, it is probable that most students will employ this, at any rate in their early studies.

CHAPTER SIX

THE
JUDGMENT OF THE HOROSCOPE :
CHARACTER

§ 1

CHARACTER and destiny interact perpetually in life. The
man of will and wisdom is able to a large extent to control
circumstance. But this is true only of his more mature years;
in childhood he necessarily endures the limitations of his
environment, and consciously and unconsciously is affected
and modified by it, while the ordinary person remains to a
large extent the passive recipient of environmental influence throughout his life.

Hence, astrologically, we cannot draw a clear line between that portion of the nativity which works out in terms
of character and that which is shown in destiny. In a general sense positions in angles tend to affect the life of physical manifestation, while the succeedent houses affect the feelings and character, and the cadent houses the mind. But it
will be found that in practice there is an infinite interblending
of action, just as there is in real life. If we find a cardinal
planet, such as Mars, in a cardinal house and sign, and ruling cardinal houses, then we may be fairly sure that his action will chiefly affect the external life. But such a conflu-
ence of planetary action is comparatively rare.

In deciding whether a given aspect will work out in terms of character or of destiny the following principles may be of value :

1. So far as character is concerned, contradictory influences tend, as life advances and the character becomes formed, to cancel out.

   Thus in children or childish adults we may find alternate good and bad temper, due perhaps to such contradictory influences as Venus rising in Libra and Moon in Scorpio. But, as the nature becomes stabilized, one or other characteristic, in all probability that which is least compatible with the needs of the environment, will die away.

2. Sidereal influences, when denied manifestation in terms of character, by reason of contradictory indications, then tend to manifest in terms of the external life, such as health, finance, reputation, etc.

   Such action does not seem to be subject to the cancelling-out principle. Thus, if the lord of the 5th were afflicted by the lord of the 2nd, but in good aspect with a planet in that house, then speculative activities would benefit from the one and suffer from the other in separate directions.

It is because of this tendency on the part of aspects to cancel out, so far as character is concerned, that it is impossible to give cut-and-dried accounts of the effects of aspects. Such might be to some extent satisfactory as applied to children or primitive adults, but they would only mislead if referred to men of ideals and progressive moral character.

§ 2. MORAL STATUS

Much has been written on the question : Can the astrologer decide from the horoscope the moral status of the native or must he be informed of this before committing himself to the task of delineation ?

Naturally this is a vital consideration, and the answer probably is, that, while he cannot legislate for exceptional cases, for Christs or Neros, yet he can as a rule judge the moral condition of the native with considerable accuracy.

For the purpose of discussing this point we can distinguish six classes, corresponding symbolically to the six celestial influences (counting the Lights as the positive and negative sides of the same influence, and omitting ♅ and ♆).

We must first distinguish two main classes :

1. Those chiefly governed by impulse, instinct, and emotion. These are the Fire-Water types.
2. Those who have reached the deliberative stage, and are governed by definite principles and purposes. These are the Air-Earth types.

Each of these classes may be subdivided as Primitive, Average, and Advanced.

The Primitive Instinctual type is represented by the Brutal Criminal, and the Primitive Deliberative type by the Cunning Criminal. These may be symbolized by Mars and

Saturn—of course, in their primitive aspect.

The average Instinctual type may be represented by the Sun-Moon, and the Average Deliberative by Mercury. It is remarkable how beautifully Astrology, with its recognition of these three influences as morally neutral — neither malefic nor benefic — coincides with this classification.

The Advanced Instinctive type is represented by the person dominated by generous emotions, i.e., the true philanthropist, symbolized by Jupiter. The Advanced Deliberative type is the true idealist, symbolized by Venus.

It is suggested that Uranus and Neptune may typify the deliberate and instinctive classes, but the natures of these planets are so complex and in some respects anomalous that a decision on this point is difficult.

Reverting to the six types given above, it will be found that a great preponderance in a horoscope of the planetary influences attributed to them will tend to produce persons of the corresponding class. Most persons, of course, belong to the Average category or present a complex of several types.

At best, much Mars and little Venus make the native inclined to roughness and little appreciation of the refinements of life.

Much Saturn and little Jupiter inclines to narrowness, lack of warmth and generosity.

On the other hand, too much Venus and Jupiter make the native too fortunate ; he is too well placed in life for his own good, and loses the power of hard work and effort. There is often childishness and irresponsibility, especially with much Libra or Pisces.

Perhaps the best sign of a good moral standard is a strong 9th house. This makes the native conscientious in the best sense, whereas, if the 9th be much afflicted, he often cares little what his actions may be, from the moral point of view.

We may usefully contrast the 5th house with the 9th—the animal impulses with the conscience. The 5th shows what we naturally, or instinctively, enjoy doing ; what we should do, were we unrestrained by moral and social considerations. Thus evil planets here, unchecked by harmonious contacts, may easily have serious results. This is particularly the case with Uranus in the 5th, because of the rebellious and self-willed influence that this planet may exert in a generally ill-controlled horoscope.

The 10th affects us through our sense of self-respect and honour.

The student must avoid the common mistake of supposing that the mere presence of many " bad " aspects will produce an evil person. This is far from being the case, though such a condition will probably indicate a difficult life, and, perhaps, many errors of judgment.

The Ruler is important. Most criminals have their rulers badly afflicted, and though all who have this horoscopic condition are not criminals, yet their moral character will probably be weak in the direction indicated by the evil influence.[1]

Prominent benefics, especially in relation to the Moon

---

[1] The reader is cautioned against taking too literally some of the descriptions given in the older style of text-books, themselves often based on older works still, which were written at a time when mankind was more prone to violent self-expression.

Remember to judge the strength of the ruler *by Sign* as well as *Aspect*. A planet in its own sign is greatly fortified.

and Mercury, all benefit the nature considerably, and it is usually found that criminals and evil-doers have all four of these bodies severely afflicted. On the other hand, high-principled people may have one or two of them afflicted.

Afflictions to the Sun should be taken as a rule as af-fecting the *outer life*, and while they may cause the native to make many mistakes and meet frequent misfortunes, they should never by themselves be considered proof of immo-rality.

Afflictions between Mars and Saturn are often stated in text-books to cause great cruelty, hardness, and even brutal-ity, but this is by no means the case, although, in a bad horoscope, they may augment such characteristics. They are, in fact, quite compatible with sweetness of temper and disposition, but in all cases they seem to destroy the finer side of the Saturn action. The native lacks the real depth of purpose and persistence of Saturn, and may be superficial or inclined to play at things ; or he may live by fits and starts, taking up things and abandoning them again too readily.

A distinction of great importance is that between per-sons with most bodies in the beginning of the zodiac and those with most bodies in the last signs. This applies par-ticularly to those with many bodies in the *first two* or *last two*. The former class tends to crude and objective expres-sion ; the latter to idealistic and subjective attitudes.

Thus the former easily produces a brutal type and the latter a dreamy unpractical one. So the criminal commonly shows many planets in Aries or Taurus and the wastrel many in Aquarius or Pisces.

Here, as in most cases, a good blend is most advantageous. The above refers only to extreme examples.

From an evolutionary standpoint one may say that the Aries-Taurus type is a primitive and at the beginning of his evolution, whilst the Aquarius-Pisces is at the end. But in either case we may get either a good or a faulty expression ; the natus shows the stage the ego is at, rather than whether or not it has mastered the lessons of that stage. Each may be good at its own work, and it is certainly pleasanter to see a good expression of the primitive than a defective expression of the evolved.

We now turn to the consideration of the disposition and temperament, apart from the question of the special degree of evolution to which the native has attained.

§ 3. GENERAL DISPOSITION AND TEMPERAMENT

Our first consideration is the *Elements*. We tabulate the number of planets in fire, air, earth, and water signs, and note any preponderance or deficiency. If there appear to be a deficiency, we see if the planetary positions help this. Thus, Mars conj. Sun will to some extent compensate for absence of planets in fire. If there is a marked deficiency or predominance, the effects will be extremely important, and will affect nearly the entire judgment, as, for example, marriage, vocation, and health. The effects of the elements are given in Chapter Four, and must be carefully studied from the life. The astrologer must learn to detect the buoyant, self-confident, hearty, or aggressive fire influence ; the shrinking, receptive, and yet tenacious water ; the plodding, patient, and often commonplace earth ; the light, humane, and friendly air. These are at work in all the objects around us, in our own minds, and in those of others, working in gross or subtle forms, harmoniously or at variance, and their action is the keynote of the Universe.

We then similarly examine the horoscope in order to detect which quality predominates, and whether we have to deal with the man of action, feeling or thought.

We may find all these well balanced, and then assume the native to be average in all respects of character, unless very powerful aspects distort the nature.

We now carefully examine the ascendant, as being the lens through which all influences must pass if they are to be manifest in the life. It is most important that there should be harmony between this and the rest of the horoscope.

If aspects are harmonious, almost any difference can be reconciled, but if the asc. does not accord with the rest of the map, and this dissimilarity is rendered acute by bad aspects, the resultant conflict is often very unfortunate, and the native finds himself at war with himself.

Thus a fire asc. tends to rush headlong into manifestation, and causes acute pain to a sensitive water horoscope, which is thrown into the battle of life against its own inner wish. If the reverse is the case, the timidity of a water asc. is a great handicap to a fire horoscope, which is continually held back by the sensitiveness of the medium through which it has to manifest.

Fire and earth illustrate a similar discord between enthusiasm and high spirits on the one hand, and common sense on the other.

Fire and air are less easily antagonized, but may come into conflict in the form of strife between the emotions and the cool, impartial judgment.

Water and air often manifest an acute struggle between the refined humane and intellectual side of the man, and the sensational or even animal side, there being usually a sordid element in the life of primitive water.

Water and earth, being entirely negative, tend in primitive maps to develop selfish and common-place characteristics; it is an uninspiring and uninspired combination; there is often no great evidence of psychological conflict or disharmony in the nature, because there is too much inertia for even discord to arise.

Air and earth in disharmony show the tension resulting from the difference between the purely intellectual and the practical aims in life. Harmonized, we should have here a man of practical worldly wisdom and also scholarly impartiality and judgment.

Next, the *Qualities.*

Too much cardinality makes the fussy, interfering busy body, unable to let well alone, always trying to manage, and, if there are afflictions in cardinal signs or angles, continually altering his mind and tactics, and giving himself and others much trouble to no purpose. The virtue of the cardinals is their energy and initiative.

Fixed signs predominant, with affliction, show stubbornness and persistence along the wrong lines, ending in disaster. The action of fixed signs is nearly always sudden and far-reaching, but may be held off for years.

If the horoscope is good, we get the man of natural power and authority, occupying a prominent and stable position.

Mutables in affliction cause irresolution, worry, bad temper, nervousness, misunderstandings, and lack of principle. Their virtues lie in their fine mental faculties and adaptability.

The next points to consider are the Rising Sign and its Ruler, any Rising Planet, the Sun, Moon and Mercury.

The *Rising Sign* is the physical body, which is the instrument by which manifestation in the material world is possible. The general characteristics of the signs are given in Chapter Four and those of the planets in Chapter Three. These descriptions will be found to apply when the signs or planets are rising, but attention must also be paid to the *Ruler*, whose importance may easily be overlooked. Much may be learnt as to the character and temperament of the native from this body, as well as of his relations with his environment. The sign and house occupied indicate his tastes and interests as well as how he is placed in life, especially in what may be styled his ordinary everyday life. Further, the aspects to the ruler denote sources of strength and weakness in character and help and hindrance in fortune. For example, if the ruler is square Neptune from the 8th house it denotes constant hindrances from matters of health, a tendency to worry, especially about 8th house matters, and perhaps certain weaknesses of character. But if Jupiter is in good aspect from the 7th, then a close friend or the marriage or business partner will be of a Jovian character and will assist and encourage him to overcome the Neptunian difficulties, and in many ways things and people denoted by Jupiter will befriend and help him, and his own nature will possess Jovian traits that will aid him.

A *Rising Planet* often seems to become as it were part-ruler and may be judged as a powerful influence that enters into the native's life and destiny for good or ill, according to its nature and strength by sign and aspect.

Planets on the M.C. are decidedly important, affecting mainly the fortunes but also the disposition and the ambitions. Some indeed hold that such planets, if very powerful, may virtually become the ruler of the horoscope.

The *Sun and Moon* represent the two poles, positive and negative, of the native's life and energy. The Sun stands for the primal vitalizing principle in the horoscope. In a woman's map its effects are often not very marked, unless she develops a strongly individual life of her own in the world of action. Otherwise they are seen chiefly in the lives of her father and husband. In a man's map it shows where the heart is, where his ambitions and cravings are, especially as regards *doing things*.

The Moon represents the more inner nature, that part of us which seeks to seclude itself, our powers not of giving or doing, but of absorbing and feeling. In a male map its effects often seem to be best seen in the life of the mother or wife.

The Sun is conscious action, the Moon is subconscious. The Sun is deliberate action, the Moon is custom and habit.

The Moon is accumulative, and this quality enables it to store up, digest and assimilate the experiences reaped by the Sun in the field of action. In this aspect, the Moon has much to do with the memory, which is the great accumulation of past experiences.

The Sun tends to denote special and outstanding events and performances; the Moon, habitual characteristics. For instance, Lord Roberts had the Sun trine Mars, and won the V.C. The Moon trine Mars would be more likely to produce the habit of courage on its more negative and passive side, such as patience and endurance.

The Sun and Moon must be most carefully studied, for they are the basis of character and destiny, and their sign- and house-positions repay the most careful attention, as do also their aspects.

Generally speaking, the Moon is the better index of moral character, while the Sun affects the fortunes and achievements of the native.

For example, Sun afflicted by Saturn shows obstacles and a hard struggle in life, but may not affect character perceptibly, while the Moon afflicted by Saturn usually denotes a timid or hard and mean element in the nature, pronounced or otherwise according to other factors.

Mercury is the intellect and also the power of self-expression, without which a man may be clever but unable to write or speak freely. While the Sun and Moon are impulsive and instinctive, Mercury is rational, and therefore, if it is strong, it may do much to assist in counteracting other dangerous tendencies. At the same time it is very open to doubt as to whether the position of this planet alone causes moral goodness or depravity, but, since it rules all intellectual expression, its afflictions denote such faults as ill-temper, narrowness or bigotry, carelessness, the tendency to backbite or criticize harshly, to slander, and so forth. Further, when the general standard of morality is low, an afflicted Mercury lends itself readily to such crimes as forgery, embezzlement, falsification of accounts, and deception of all sorts.

We now pass to a tabulation of the general effects attributable to planets in signs, bearing in mind that such effects are modified by house and aspect and can really only be considered in the widest sense unless the student has an actual map before him. These effects are most marked in the case of the Sun, Moon, Ruler, and Mercury, but they apply to some extent to all planets.

SUN IN

ARIES .... Bold, energetic, generous, stubborn.

TAURUS .... Slow, conservative, very fixed.

GEMINI .... Quick, changeable, perhaps shallow.

CANCER .... Retiring and often a prey to moods ; much shrewdness and common sense.

LEO .... A generous, large-minded, capable nature.

VIRGO .... Gentlemanly, accomplished, quiet dignity, hard-working and thorough.

LIBRA .... Disputatious, liable to suffer through associates.

SCORPIO .... Proud, unyielding, dignified, sometimes over-bearing.

SAGITTARIUS ... Cheerful, restless, frank, and generous, courteous, and dignified.

CAPRICORN ..... Dignified, ambitious, controlled, purposive.

AQUARIUS .... Artistic and gifted, peculiar, but sincere and honest ; unfortunate through associates unless Sun is strong.

PISCES .... Good-natured, kind, hospitable, easy-going.

MOON IN

ARIES .... Quick, excitable, pushing, easily roused.

TAURUS .... Contented, practical, common-sense, reliable, easy-going, pleasure-loving.

GEMINI .... Active mentally and physically, often brilliant, hard, variable.

CANCER .... Sensitive, retiring, shrewd, changeful, but sympathetic and protective.

MOON IN

LEO	Kind, affectionate, emotional, fond of pleasure.
VIRGO	Businesslike and industrious, but often meticulous and fussy; small self-confidence.
LIBRA	Charming, sympathetic, sociable, and happy.
SCORPIO	A moody, repressed nature, given to brooding ; easily injured and made jealous ; often rough and crude.
SAGITTARIUS	Frank, jolly, changeable, and rather superficial.
CAPRICORN	Cold, suspicious, over-cautious, thrifty.
AQUARIUS	Inquisitive, humane, tolerant, friendly.
PISCES	Negative and receptive, easily swayed, kind and affectionate.

MERCURY IN

ARIES	A fiery, disputatious person, easily exaggerates.
TAURUS	Self-opinionated, conventional, limited in interests.
GEMINI	Very quick, mentally fluent, and talkative ; dispassionate, rather selfish.
CANCER	Loquacious, emotional, changeable ; the memory is good, and there is a tendency to live in the past.
LEO	A firm, determined, rather self-satisfied person.
VIRGO	Neat, quiet, business-like, and matter-of-fact.
LIBRA	Accomplished, scholarly, social, amusing.
SCORPIO	A deep, silent, repressed person, acute and penetrating.
SAGITTARIUS	Loquacious, shallow, small concentration, careless of detail.
CAPRICORN	Practical, often eloquent and clever ; dissatisfied.
AQUARIUS	Scientific, inquisitive, humane.
PISCES	Mentally confused, absent-minded, kindly, often artistic and humorous.

VENUS IN

ARIES	Attractive, but restless, impressionable, and fickle.
TAURUS	Musical, artistic, pleasant, social.
GEMINI	Kind, clever, artistic, very gifted in self-expression.
CANCER	Much sympathy, protectiveness, and homely charm.
LEO	Affectionate and warm nature, fond of the good things of life.
VIRGO	Tidy, precise, rather exacting.
LIBRA	Much charm of manner and disposition ; a sweet and gentle nature.

VENUS IN

SCORPIO .... Intense, highly sensitive to neglect or slights ; exacting and jealous.

SAGITTARIUS ... Affectionate, demonstrative, changeful.

CAPRICORN ..... Sincere and honourable, conventional, sometimes inclined to snobbishness and worldliness.

AQUARIUS .... An idealistic, refined nature ; love for the society of friends.

PISCES .... Very affectionate, often too easy-going, and easily influenced.

MARS IN

ARIES .... A vigorous, dominant, autocratic nature ; unable to compromise or give way ; great energy and courage.

TAURUS .... An ill-tempered nature ; extreme obstinacy.

GEMINI .... Argumentative, acute, brilliant.

CANCER .... Often moody, quarrelsome, but not courageous ; great tenacity.

LEO .... A powerful personality ; generous, hot-tempered, self-willed.

VIRGO .... A good practical worker ; thorough and painstaking ; apt to be very critical of others.

LIBRA .... Amiable and often charming, but liable to be lazy and easy-going ; lacks self-reliance.

SCORPIO .... Strong, dignified, intense and enduring emotions ; self-contained.

SAGITTARIUS ... Frank, extremely active, full of fun and spirits ; apt to be extravagant and over-ready to run after new ideas.

CAPRICORN ..... A proud, vigorous, decided character ; restless, and hates subordination.

AQUARIUS .... Scientific and cultured, high-principled.

PISCES .... Easily played upon by others ; emotional, restless, often resentful and discontented.

JUPITER IN

ARIES .... Active, high-spirited, self-willed and liberty-loving.

TAURUS .... Pleasure-loving, indolent, self-indulgent ; little inspiration.

GEMINI .... Clever, but often superficial ; credulous or sceptical in turn.

CANCER .... Kind, sympathetic, genuine, and good.

LEO .... A magnanimous disposition ; full of helpfulness and affection.

VIRGO .... Quiet, critical, kind, but narrow in the affections ; matter-of-fact, often conceited.

LIBRA .... Good, just, sociable, artistic, or scientific.

SCORPIO .... Reserved, dignified, sometimes reckless or self-indulgent ; may be conceited.

JUPITER IN

SAGITTARIUS ... A high-spirited, liberty-loving, generous, good-natured person ; often reckless ; lacking in concentration of effort.

CAPRICORN ..... Reticent, self-controlled, righteous, and conscientious, sometimes puritanic or austere.

AQUARIUS .... Just, humane, considerate, and often gifted in science.

PISCES .... Jolly, pleasant, easy-going, friendly, and devoted to philanthropy and public work.

SATURN IN

ARIES .... Apt to lack true depth ; careless and irresponsible ; alternately weak and strong.

TAURUS .... Matter-of-fact ; may be lethargic, dull, and selfish.

GEMINI .... A serious, profound mind ; cold, impartial, and scientific.

CANCER .... A melancholy, repining nature ; often clannish, suspicious, mean, and timid.

LEO .... Reserved, and in some way the nature is stunted, and the feelings denied outlet.

VIRGO .... Careful, practical, conscientious, often severe on others.

LIBRA .... A serious, but pleasant nature, often much spirituality and other-worldliness.

SCORPIO .... Suspicious, proud, restrained, much will-power and endurance.

SAGITTARIUS ... Honourable, grave, dignified, often very capable.

CAPRICORN ..... Able in affairs, materialistic or formal in regard to religion; limited, persistent, careful, and calculating ; highly ambitious.

AQUARIUS .... Scientific, careful, mentally conscientious, humane, exact.

PISCES .... A sad, moody disposition ; much sorrow and disappointment ; his own enemy.

URANUS IN

ARIES .... Self-willed, proud, extremely courageous, rebellious, vituperative, dogmatic.

TAURUS .... Selfish, immovable, ill-humoured.

GEMINI .... Very gifted, original, and able ; inventive and versatile.

CANCER .... Eccentric, very uncertain and strange.

LEO .... An unfortunate position, often producing uncontrollable emotional storms and hysteria ; eccentric.

VIRGO .... Inventive, original, clever, whimsical.

LIBRA .... Romantic, restless, uncertain ; often scientific.

URANUS IN

SCORPIO .... Concentrated emotions ; may be malicious and revengeful, and sensitive to supposed injustice or neglect.

SAGITTARIUS ... Rebellious, excitable, highly strung, and reckless.

CAPRICORN ..... Pushing, restless, dominating, a good organizer and leader, but useless as a servant.

AQUARIUS .... Clever, humane, scientific.

PISCES .... Very unsettled, intermittent, and changeful.

NEPTUNE IN

ARIES .... A schemer ; often a subtle, subversive, and dangerous character ; in a good horoscope, idealistic.

TAURUS .... Musical, kind, charming.

GEMINI .... Fanciful, delicate mentality ; often rather peevish and worrying.

CANCER .... Dreamy, mediumistic, lazy.

LEO .... Unreliable, attractive, but weak ; inflated idea of own value.

VIRGO .... Very critical, and apt to find fault.

LIBRA .... Visionary, romantic, subtly attractive.

SCORPIO .... Likely to be extremely subtle, and possibly cruel.

SAGITTARIUS ... Aspiring, visionary, utopian.

CAPRICORN ..... A calculating and scheming character.

AQUARIUS .... Much idealism and desire to benefit humanity.

PISCES .... Gentle, artistic, and loving ; much love of the weak and poor.

NOTE. – It is, of course, impossible to have personal knowledge of people born with Neptune rising in each of the signs, and to a lesser extent this also applies to Uranus. Data from the past are also not always available, and some of the foregoing delineations are therefore, as regards these planets, entirely hypothetical.

§ 4. INTELLECTUAL ABILITIES

These cannot be judged from Mercury, for this planet rules self-expression rather than actual brain-power. If strong, it nearly always gives fluency with tongue and pen, but it may also be mentally shallow and flippant. On the other hand, a good Saturn gives good judgment, sense, and wisdom, in contradistinction to cleverness.

Uranus in good aspect to either planet may give exceptional talent.

General mental ability seems (in contradiction to the usual belief) to be most clearly indicated by good *solar* aspects, especially to ♂, ♃ or ♅.

Aspects to the asc. affect the brain, regarded as the physical vehicle for mental expression, and weaken and strengthen it according to their nature.

Many bodies in mutables make the mind active, often with a thirst for knowledge, especially the two positives. Virgo may be conservative and conventional. Pisces is artistic rather than strictly mental.

Virgo rising, with a group of planets in Gemini, as in the case of the Duke of Marlborough, may give a very fine mentality.

The Moon in good aspect to Mercury makes for mental carefulness and soundness. It is an excellent position for a business man.

Finally, we must mention the 3rd house as frequently affecting the mind very noticeably. Afflictions to it account for most mental affections, such as mental deficiency, dulness, depressions, delusions, morbid fears, and, combined with other heavy afflictions, insanity.

Other things being equal, we may say :

The Sun herein renders the mind strong, self-reliant, and as a rule literary and accomplished.

The Moon causes a dreamy, imaginative, and moody mentality.

Mercury denotes a quick, bright, and witty mind.

Venus improves the disposition, and denotes a kind, courteous, and accomplished mind.

Mars may, if much afflicted, give temper, and indicates an excitable or even hysterical tendency, especially if in water. If strong, there is aptitude for argument and dispute, and the native will more readily perceive differences than agreements between his own ideas and those of others.

Jupiter generally improves the disposition, but detracts somewhat from the purely mental and logical side of the mind. It may show conceit.

Saturn, if strong, gives care, exactness, and conscientiousness to the mental attitude. If weak, there may be melancholy, hardness, narrowness of mental outlook, and even stupidity.

Uranus is well placed as a rule in the 3rd, and gives an original and very active mind.

Neptune, if strong, favours a mystical or artistic character, but when weak may cause much trouble, and inclines to some sort of deception or muddle.

These configurations must be collated with the position of Mercury, the accidental ruler of the 3rd, and other significators of character, but their presence can usually be readily detected.

It must be added that very good horoscopical positions are as a rule not so good, nor very bad always so bad, as would often at first sight appear. There seems to be a certain principle of reaction in nature which tends to bring such cases towards the normal.

As an example of this one may cite the natus of the Prince Consort, who was born with Mercury rising in Virgo in major bad aspects with all four malefics from angles. It had no good aspects. Jupiter was almost as weak. The Sun and Moon were in sextile, but had no other good aspects, and only Venus was at all well placed, even she being ca-

dent. The astrologer might easily draw from such a horoscope a gloomy picture, not only of worldly failure, but of
mental and moral depravity. Yet the native was a conscientious, enlightened, and accomplished man ; he wedded a
great monarch, and his married life was certainly far from
entirely unhappy. His early unpopularity and premature
death seem the chief results of these afflictions.

Afflictions may act as incentives to a powerful and
healthy character, whilst " good " configurations may prove
temptations to a weak one, inducing it to waste time in self-
indulgence and puerilities.

§ 5. The Effects of the Aspects[1]

The next consideration is that of the effects of aspects,
regarded as influences modifying the planets and so altering
their action in respect of character.

The following notes are studied from life, and should
prove helpful to the beginner if read in a wide sense and
studied in relation to the more general and deeper psychological issues of the nativity. An attempt to apply them too
rigidly, wide as they are, would probably lead to serious
misjudgments, apparent if not real. The actual effect delin-
eated might indeed exist in the character, but if overlaid by
contrary influences it might easily escape the notice of the
native's friends, or even his own, unless he were by training

---

[1] These are treated in detail in the author's book *The Astrological Aspects*.

or instinct an acute observer of the inner processes of his mind and feelings.

The notes are based on the permanent, or essential, natures of the heavenly bodies. It is impossible to compile accounts of their influences as differentiated by sign, aspect, and house, for such would run into many thousands. The task, therefore, of adapting each description according to the other factors embodied in each horoscope must be left to the intuition of the student. Astrological delineation is not, and cannot be treated as, a cut-and-dried matter.

The essential natures of the aspecting planets, modified by the signs occupied and the aspects received from other bodies, determine the exact nature of the aspect, which will then seek expression through the houses occupied.

It should be understood that all good aspects tend to bring benefits through the things ruled essentially by the planets in aspect, and trouble if they are in bad aspect. For example, any good aspect to Jupiter will tend to bring benefit through law, foreign affairs, sports, or some other Jovian matter. We must ask the reader to bear this in mind, for it would be a waste of space to repeat it throughout.

The Sun often operates through the father, especially in youth, and, in a woman's horoscope through the husband. Similarly, the Moon stands for the mother, and, in male maps, the wife. Mercury often stands for boys and young people ; Venus for young women ; Mars for young men ; and Saturn for the aged.

Planets in dignity often perform much good even by bad aspect, especially the benefics, and contrariwise planets debili-

*tated cannot be relied on for great benefits, especially the ma-
lefics, whatever aspects they may form.*[1]

	THE SUN	
In Aspect with	*In Good Aspect.*	*In Bad Aspect.*
The Moon..................	Very wide in effect, benefits business, health, and home. The nature is harmonious.	Generally unfortunate, though in a wide rather than a specific sense. Home-disturbances ; the recuperative powers are poor. Heart and digestion may suffer.
Mercury	The ♂ is thought undesirable by some. The memory is good ; some pride and a self-opinionated tendency.	None formed.
Venus	The ♂ adds to the refinement and artistic ability, but may occasion some degree of affectation and effeminacy.	Only the ∠ is possible. It causes some trouble with the affections. They are too easily stimulated ; there may be carelessness and a prodigal tendency.
Mars	A courageous, energetic, and vigorous nature. Success in all matters under the planet. Good for all investigatory work. Often good brain-power, especially with the ✶.	The same, but impetuous, self-willed, extreme emotionally, militant, and even violent. Wastes energy and feelings Liability to illness or accident under bad directions.

---

[1]There is, perhaps, a rather common tendency to place too little importance on sign-position and too much on aspects.

JUDGMENT OF THE HOROSCOPE: CHARACTER

THE SUN

In Aspect with	In Good Aspect.	In Bad Aspect.
Jupiter	Generous, sincere, honourable, philanthropic, fond of sport, and, in later years, religion or philosophy. A fine testimony to success and health. Prudent yet progressive. Good intellectual powers.	Apt to be involved in unprofitable relations with all Jovian things. May be wasteful, over-hopeful, apt to take risks and lack prudence.
Saturn	Honest hard-working, careful, persistent, tactful, and ambitious. Gain by steady effort and sober merit. Help from those older and more highly placed.	Unfortunate in most undertakings, many checks and frequent opposition or bad luck. In females usually prevents or much delays marriage and children. Much trouble with old people and those in authority. Misfortunes to the father.
Uranus	An original, energetic mind, dominant and fond of responsibility and leadership ; often magnetic and powerful personality. Broadminded ; unhampered by convention, drastic.	Clever but perverse, selfwilled and stubborn, often against own interests. Tactless, easily roused to opposition and liable to make many enemies and meet with sudden reverses. Highly strung nerves.
Neptune	Often bestows much good fortune, but affects the character little, except that it may bestow a subtle tendency and love of secrecy.	Loss and worry through confused and treacherous conditions ; the native may get himself into bad muddles ; he is utopian and unpractical; may be himself irresponsible, foolish, and even tricky.

THE MOON

In Aspect with	In Good Aspect.	In Bad Aspect.
Mercury	Greatly quickens and improves the mind ; accurate, careful, seldom makes slips. Strengthens brain and nerves.	Clever but careless. A tendency to gossip and backbite. The nerves are often affected.
Venus	Much affection ; a kind, gentle, harmonious, and happy disposition. A happy marriage. Artistic abilities.	Apt to produce slackness, untidiness, and indolence, especially in regard to domestic matters. Affectionate but often silly or childish.
Mars	A quick, practical, decisive temperament ; robust and vigorous health.	Rough, and sometimes ill-tempered or immoral.
Jupiter	Adds greatly to the generosity, sympathy, and warmth of the nature. A truly kind, helpful, and philanthropic nature. Excellent for social and financial advancement.	Trouble through Jovian matters. Careless and extravagant.
Saturn	Thrift, prudence, steadiness, carefulness and perseverance. Cool, self-contained, self-controlled, hard-working.	Great closeness with money, suspicion, timidity, apprehension. Often selfish and narrow. Inefficient.
Uranus	Often gives some psychic ability, such as psychometry, automatic writing. Unexpected benefits.	Nervous troubles. The temper is uncertain, rebellious and resentful ; eccentric.
Neptune	Dreamy, imaginative, and bohemian.	Irresponsible, unpractical, muddling ; often critical and a fault-finder.

MERCURY

In Aspect with	In Good Aspect.	In Bad Aspect.
Venus	The ♂ is one of the best indications of an harmonious, refined, and gentle nature, with a very polished and agreeable manner. Very favourable for artistic work. The ✳ is the same, but less strong.	The ∠ has small effect, but may cause trouble in regard to the things essentially ruled by the planets.
Mars	The mind is sharp, quick, active, able to seize points ; a good debater and hard mental worker.	The same, but there is a tendency to be quarrelsome, sarcastic, exaggerative, and careless. There is a danger of mental strain and breakdown. In bad maps, reckless and dishonest.
Jupiter	Prudent, thoughtful, just, and kind ; a very understanding mind and good judgment.	Exaggerative, over-optimistic, apt to make mistakes and to be careless about details. Sceptical or superstitious.
Saturn	A quiet, careful, conscientious mind ; often a deep and serious turn of thought. Exact and matter-of-fact, logical, and clear.	Narrowness of outlook often hardness and cruelty. Depression. A laborious, pedantic tendency ; lack of originality.
Uranus	Clear, original, humorous; brilliant, but often unfitted for routine work; scientific or artistic.	Original, but often eccentric or perverse.
Neptune	Poetic, musical, inspirational ; often mystical tendencies ; subtle and and delicate mind.	Illusive, bohemian, unpractical ; often self-deceived.

121

VENUS

In Aspect with	In Good Aspect.	In Bad Aspect.
Mars	Feelings and affections are very easily roused, demonstrative ; fond of enjoyment.	Separation from the object of the affections ; active and sensitive emotions, lack of interior peace and concord ; unhappy childhood.
Jupiter	Benefits the social and moral nature, a genial, social person ; slight effect on the external life.	Careless, self-indulgent, restless, vain, sometimes revolutionary ; often an excess of feeling.
Saturn	Benefits from the aged. Constant and steady affections.	The affections are centred on a very small circle, and are apt to be selfish and exacting. Bereavement and sorrow.
Uranus	Often very attractive and fascinating ; artistic and tasteful ; romantic.	Romantic, but unfortunate in romance, and often forms attachments of an irregular nature ; jealous, uncertain.
Neptune	A very beautiful and spiritual nature ; artistic and poetic. In primitive maps this will have small effect.	Much worry and instability in regard to the affections. Disillusion. The native may have high ideals which are not realized. There may be deception, both in love and finance.

MARS

In Aspect with	In Good Aspect.	In Bad Aspect.
Jupiter	Enthusiasm and energy in all Jovian matters ; generous and enterprising, but prudent in undertakings.	Wasteful, extravagant, too hopeful ; imprudent, often a gambler ; may be foolishly enthusiastic about wrong causes ; a sectary.

MARS

In Aspect with	In Good Aspect.	In Bad Aspect.
Saturn	A practical, materialistic character, often severe and without appreciation of the finer elements of life.	A hard nature in a bad map; otherwise a lack of true responsibility, inconstancy in carrying out plans. Fitful. Liable to strain and over-work.
Uranus	Physical energy and much muscular strength. A powerful and dominant character.	Often an ungoverned temper. Danger of accidents. A waste of energy.
Neptune	Strong and deep emotions; an unusual power of insight and penetration.	May give suffering from deceit or vice. Obsessions, fears, danger from liquids. Very active imagination.

JUPITER

In Aspect with	In Good Aspect.	In Bad Aspect.
Saturn	Steady common sense and ability ; a serious, thoughtful, and stable nature. An excellent augury of enduring success.	Unlucky, lack of enterprise and initiative or else of persistence ; narrow or depressing religious views.
Uranus	Great originality, and sometimes mental powers much above the ordinary.	Perverted or misguided ability ; dishonesty or rebelliousness ; waywardness, lack of self-discipline ; many erroneous ideas.
Neptune	Very humane, philanthropic, sympathetic, hospitable and fond of succouring the weak. Spiritual and mystical.	Self-deception or hypocrisy. Indifference to religion, or else superstitious. Very emotional. Undependable unless ♄ is strong.

SATURN

In Aspect with	*In Good Aspect.*	*In Bad Aspect.*
Uranus	A union of will and persistence, common sense and originality.	The originality is limited for expression or may be perverted into stubbornness and persistence in following wrong tracks.
Neptune	Probably assists much to make the ideals concrete and practical. Common sense and self-control ; powers of organizing. Diplomatic.	The spiritual development is inhibited. Sometimes coldness, cruelty or cynicism. Friends may be deceptive or parasitic.

URANUS

In Aspect with	*In Good Aspect.*	*In Bad Aspect.*
Neptune	Interests in occult and psychic matters.	The same, but a liability to mistakes and delusive beliefs.

IMPORTANT NOTE

Do not forget that too much stress must never be laid on *wide* aspects. It is those that are exact to within a degree or less that really operate vigorously, especially if they fall near a cusp.

CHAPTER SEVEN

THE
JUDGMENT OF THE HOROSCOPE :
DESTINY

IN this Chapter we must consider, from the twelve houses and the indications affecting them by sign and planet, what the lot of the native is likely to be in respect of health, finance, and other more or less external matters. At the same time we cannot too closely lay to heart that character and destiny are largely inseparable. At times we may believe we have found a temperamental trait that has affected nothing in the outer life, and more often we shall be tempted to say that some event that has befallen ourselves or another "had nothing whatever to do with character". But the more closely we examine such cases the more careful we become of making such assertions.

In more advanced text-books the reader will often find the questions of destiny treated in great detail and at considerable length. The influence of each planet in each house is considered, and often numerous aphorisms, many of them dating from medieval and earlier times, are added. These are of much use if read as suggestions, and they often teach the beginner a great deal and may put him on the right track. But so complex is the horoscope that it rarely happens that these descriptions are correct in word and spirit. Mars in the 2nd in Cancer is very different from Mars in 2nd in

Leo, and even if it be in the same sign in each of two cases, a trine of Jupiter in one and a square of the Sun in the other may alter the apparent result altogether. *Hence the student should strive above all to master the real meanings or ideas underlying the factors of Astrology and should try to apply them for himself.* He will find many difficult problems, for life is full of complications, paradoxes and surprises ; we understand little of ourselves and less of others. But when he has acquired experience he will find that he can trust Astrology as he can trust nothing else.

§ 1. HEALTH AND DEATH

Physical well-being depends upon the two Luminaries, the asc., and the 6th and 8th houses, as well as, to some extent, the 4th and the 12th. All configurations that involve any of these are liable to affect the health.

Tradition teaches that one of the Lights or the asc. is *Hyleg* in every map, this being an Arabian term indicating the giver of life or the special arbitrator of life and death. According to some views the hyleg is not concerned with health as such, but with longevity, so that, for example, if the 6th were badly afflicted and the hyleg strong, the health would be bad, but the native would live long, whereas, if the reverse were the case, the health would be good, but life would be short, perhaps owing to an accident.

Furthermore, opinions differ as to the correct method of selecting the hyleg. Some claim that the Sun is always hyleg ; others take the Sun for males and Moon for females.

The common rule, adapted and simplified from that given by Claudius Ptolemy, the father of western astrology, is as follows :—

The following areas are denominated " hylegiacal ", namely, the 1st, 7th, 9th, and 10th houses, and the half of the 11th nearest the M.C. If the Sun is therein, it is hyleg ; if it is not, but the Moon is, she is hyleg ; if neither is, the asc. is taken. Some take ⊕ if the Lights are not in hylegiacal places, the asc. only being used if all three are not so situated.

The examination of a few dozen cases of early death or, on the other hand, of examples of marked longevity, will probably cause the student to entertain grave doubts on the whole question of the hyleg, for it is not hard to find cases where death seems certainly due to a violent affliction to a luminary well removed from hylegiacal positions, and instances are also found where the native has attained great age with the hyleg violently afflicted.

Moreover, the question arises as to whether the hyleg remains the same through life, or changes as the horoscope progresses (see Chapter Ten).

The 4th house rules the end of life, and if Jupiter is therein, or if this planet (and sometimes Uranus or Neptune) is in strong good aspect to the lord or occupant of this house, it is perhaps as good an indication as any of a long and healthy old age.

It is generally thought that the Sun is most important in a man's map, and the Moon in a woman's, while the latter is always important in childhood, irrespective of sex.

Lunar afflictions often work out largely through wife or mother in a man's nativity, and in a woman's the Sun's aspects often act largely through the father and husband, as we have already said.

The Moon governs the functional health and the Sun the constitution, the complaints resulting from solar afflictions being as a rule far more deep-rooted.

If the Sun, Moon, and asc. (the three hylegiacals) are not badly afflicted, the physical well-being should be assured. The stronger they are the better. Mixed aspects, good and bad, cause varying conditions. If the Luminaries are afflicted in or from angles the results are likely to be the more drastic.

Interplanetary aspects, i.e., not involving ☉, ☽ or cusps of houses, even if involving the 6th and 8th houses, do not usually cause serious trouble unless one or more of these three points be afflicted. Indeed, there is some reason to discount the value of the 6th and 8th from the health standpoint, unless the hylegiacals are involved. But if these latter are aspected from one of these houses, the effects, whether good or evil, will be especially important from the point of view of bodily welfare.

The physical rulerships of the planets are as follows :—

The Sun .... General vitality and constitutional strength. The heart and back.

The Moon .... The nutritive and assimilative system. The stomach.

Mercury .... Nerves and respiratory system.

Venus .... Kidneys, throat, skin.

Mars .... Muscular and excretory systems. Nose and nasal passages ; skull and face.

Jupiter .... The blood and liver.

Saturn .... The bones.

Uranus and Neptune .... These both work chiefly through the nervous system, but little is known with any certainty as to their physiological rulerships.

Most diseases have been found, by modern astrological research, to be due to the combined action of two or more bodies, so that most statements as to a disease being due to one planet or sign are only partially true. It is often found that one hylegiacal is usually afflicted in one disease and another in another, while in one case planetary influence may act by the planet and in another by its sign.

Thus, cancer is nearly always indicated by the Sun being in relation to Jupiter and Saturn, but this need not be by its being in aspect to both. It may be in aspect to Jupiter in or from a Saturn sign, or *vice versa.*

Again, it has been found that many diseases are specially related to certain zodiacal areas, sometimes of a very limited extent. Many of these are published for the first time in the writer's *Encyclopaedia of Psychological Astrology.*

The following traditional sign-rulerships are given subject to the above remarks :

Aries .... Head and face.
Taurus .... Neck, throat, and larynx.
Gemini .... Shoulders, arms, lungs, nervous system.
Cancer .... Stomach.
Leo .... Spine, back, and heart.
Virgo .... Bowels and fingers.
Libra .... Kidneys, lumbar region, skin.
Scorpio .... Urinary organs and lower bowel.
Sagittarius .... Hips, thighs, buttocks.
Capricorn .... Bones, knees.
Aquarius .... Ankles. Circulation.
Pisces .... Feet.

So far as diseases can be ascribed to single planets the following are characteristic maladies :

Mercury .... Neurasthenia, epilepsy, nervous excitability.
Venus .... Diseases resulting from easy and self-indulgent living. Most forms of kidney-trouble.

Mars	All feverish conditions, inflammation, sudden, acute, and painful complaints, usually resulting from strain, exhaustion, over-work, or carelessness.
Jupiter	Diseases of excess and plethora, such as gout. Abnormal growths. Complaints commonly arise from rich living and need treatment by fasting, hard exercise, and self-denial.
Saturn	Diseases are chronic and inhibitive rather than painful (unless Mars is involved as well, as in rheumatic fever). They generally result from poor living, exposure, hardships, or hereditary troubles. Rheumatism is usually shown mainly by an affliction to asc. from this planet. Melancholia.
Uranus	Sudden attacks, usually hard to foresee and to cure. The nerves are usually affected. Paralysis is mainly Uranian.
Neptune	Extreme physical sensitiveness. Morbid fears, delusions, and other obscure psychic conditions. Liability to nervous worry.

From the standpoint of general vitality the fire signs are reckoned the strongest, although Sagittarius is liable to accidents and Leo is rather commonly occupied hylegiacally in horoscopes of death at birth. The air signs come next. They are less robust, but they usually lead careful lives, although there is a liability to nervous exhaustion. Among the earthy signs, Virgo is the strongest and often exercises and diets carefully ; Taurus tends to be lazy and self-indulgent ; Capricorn is often weak as a child, but, once well started, lives long. Scorpio is the strongest of the watery signs, but is very liable to infection, and suffers much from bronchial and throat troubles, as well as appendicitis. It, too, is often delicate in infancy. Cancer and Pisces are deemed weak.

Note that the signs on the 6th and 8th cusps often affect the health, even if no planet is in them. Thus Libra suffers as much from the throat as Taurus, because it has that sign on the 8th, and Scorpio seems more liable to bronchitis than Gemini, because it has that sign on the same cusp.

It also happens at times that afflictions seem to work out " by polarity ", i.e., through the opposite signs, or even those in square with them. Thus Scorpio is the sign of diphtheria quite as much as is Taurus. All cardinals tend to affect the head, stomach, kidneys, and bones ; all fixed signs the throat, heart and trunk, genitals and circulation ; and all mutables the nerves, lungs, limbs, and bowels.

The Houses and Health

Generally speaking, the houses have the same values from the physiological standpoint as the corresponding signs, although certain diseases are particularly connected with the former, and others with the latter. For example, mental deficiency and insanity are nearly, if not always, shown by afflictions to the 3rd house, but not necessarily to Gemini, while pneumonia is normally shown by the sign Gemini, and not by the 3rd. Other diseases are particularly planetary. Mercury is often well placed in maps of mental deficiency, but nearly always badly afflicted in insanity. In fact, each disease requires careful study, founded on the examination of sufficiently numerous and reliable instances. Such investigation would add greatly to our understanding both of disease and Astrology.

Infant Mortality

One of the commonest features in the maps of children dead or dying at birth is a malefic exactly on the 4th or 7th cusp in affliction with a hylegiacal, but any affliction to one of these in or from any angle (even if not on the cusp) is highly critical unless powerful benefic influences intervene. Even then, debilitated benefics (i.e., in fall or detriment, or retrograde) must not be relied upon.

Squares between the 10th and 12th or 4th and 6th are very bad, and, if in mutables, the child will have difficulty in establishing respiration.

All three hylegiacals in negative signs seem a common feature of such maps, although Leo often contains one of them.

It is a bad sign if the ruler of the 1st is afflicted in the 8th, or *vice versa*, at least if it is a malefic, but this may by itself only show ill-health.[1]

Moon close to ♂ Sun is considered a weak position, and if a malefic afflict both it is naturally very critical.

Malefics rising are always likely to cause trouble, whereas benefics help to preserve.

Death [2]

The time of death is only to be found by a careful study of " directions " (see Chapter Ten), and then not always with certainty, or anything approaching it. Thus, the most extreme care must be observed in giving judgment on this matter, for the responsibility involved is great.

It may be said :—

If there be a malefic in the 8th, or one of the Lights badly afflicted, then its arrival by progression to the cusp of

---

[1] If it is so placed, but not afflicted at all, it would probably show one much concerned with sickness, as a nurse or doctor.

[2] This subject is exhaustively treated in the author's work *Symbolic Directions in Modern Astrology*, Chapter IV.

that house, and later its reaching the opposition of the asc., are critical periods.

The arrival of any malefic on an angle is a critical period, according to the general tenor of the map.

If the Sun is afflicted by a malefic at birth, its arrival at the next major bad aspect by direction is critical. Thus, if it is square Saturn at birth, it will reach the ♁. about forty-five years later.

If two malefics mutually afflict, then the arrival of the Sun or asc. at such a place as is in affliction with both at once, marks a dangerous time.

Similarly, many nativities show areas which are under affliction from several bodies radically ; such areas are significant of a critical period in the life, should the Sun or asc. have to pass them. The Moon's directions are much less important.

Death is usually denoted by a series of bad directions, without the interposal of any strong good influence.

§ 2. RELATIVES, MARRIAGE, AND FRIENDS

The 3rd, 7th, and 11th houses, corresponding to the three airy signs, are all connected with relationships and show, by their rulers and occupants, with what sort of people the native will be brought into contact, and with what results.

The 3rd indicates the brothers and sisters, and, according to some, other near relations. These are, however, best judged as follows :—

Aunts and uncles on father's side, as being brethren of the father : 6th ;

Aunts and uncles on the mother's side ; 12th ;

First cousins : the 5th houses from these, i.e., 4th and
10th ;

and other relations in the same manner. Such judgments
cannot, however, be carried very far, and must only be taken
to apply to the persons in question in their relation to the
native, and not as absolutely true of them as individuals.
Otherwise all children of the same parents would have to
be born with similar indications in respect of parents, aunts,
cousins, etc.

It is probably correct to take the 3rd as denoting especially the eldest brother, the 5th (i.e., third from 3rd) as the
second, and the 7th as the third, and so on, omitting those
who, by reason of early death or separation, have not influenced the native.[1]

Marriage

Venus and the 7th house stand for unions of all sorts,
and especially that of marriage. The children and the pro-
creative instinct are shown by the 5th, and this house also
rules courtship and love-making ; so soon, however, as the
marriage-tie is formed, whether legally or merely by mutual agreement, the 7th house is the controlling influence.

In its widest sense it represents all that is complementary to our personal selves, shown by the asc., all that we
lack and seek in others in order to supplement our deficiency. It is the house of all yearnings and seekings after the
unattainable or the far distant ; the house of the ideal as

---

[1] The subject of blood-relationships is a difficult one. Much depends on the
nature of the psychological bond between the native and his brothers and sisters.
It is obvious that the 3rd cannot indicate all the brothers and sisters, since these
will have different, and sometimes very different, nativities.

opposed to the actual, shown by the asc.

Astrologically we very rarely find two persons born under the same sign to be desirous of marrying one another, and this is readily understandable in the light of what has been said. The ideal, astrologically, is rather that there should be strong points of similarity in the maps of marriage partners, but at the same time points of contrast, in order that each may learn from the other and absorb some of his or her different habits of thoughts and body. Where there is strong similarity and little contrast the couple may often tire of merely being wedded to a counterpart of each other, and even if this does not happen, the lack of contrast may cause the married life to be dull and mentally and emotionally stagnant.

The commonest and strongest tie between a man and woman is probably the presence in the one horoscope of the Sun, Moon, or Venus on the asc. of the other. Such positions occasion very strong physical attraction.

The interchange of the positions of the Lights, i.e., the Sun in one placed on the Moon in the other, makes for deep sympathy and understanding.

Every near correspondence of position in two maps of persons brought into close contact will work out in some way, according to planet, sign, and house.

It is generally said that persons born under signs in square with one another should not marry, owing to the difference of element. This rule cannot by any means be considered absolute, for if the signs in this case are of different elements they are yet of the same quadruplicity. Never-

theless the marriage of two persons with very different pre-
ponderances of quality or element is likely to be somewhat
risky, although, if successful, it will probably benefit both.

A person who has much fire is likely to wear out emotionally one who is chiefly air, and physically one who is
Cancer or Pisces, and so forth.

The general circumstances of the marriage are shown
by the 7th house, and by *the application of the appropriate
Luminary*. The Sun stands for the male sex in a woman's
horoscope, and the Moon for the female in a man's, and the
first application of these bodies denotes the kind of mar-
riage-partner and the conditions of marriage. This often
works out with great exactness, the planet to which the Light
first applies being commonly the ruler or rising planet in
the natus of the partner. The theory often propounded that
the successive applications of the luminaries denote successive attachments, and that marriage takes place when, having run the gamut of any bad aspects that it may form, the
Light reaches its first good one, must be received with caution.

If the Luminary appropriate to the case apply by good
aspect to a planet, it is probable that marriage will take place
readily to a person denoted by that body, whatever subsequent applications may be made. If it apply to a benefic or
neutral by square or opposition marriage will probably ensue, but will be attended by some trouble, as shown by sign
and house. If the application be by bad aspect to a malefic,
either no marriage or an unhappy one must be expected.
Saturn is more likely to deny or greatly delay marriage, Mars
to hurry it with regrettable consequences.

JUDGMENT OF THE HOROSCOPE: DESTINY

The 7th house has a wider significance, embracing all partnerships or relationships between the native and individuals. It is possible that the general conditions of marriage are shown by this house, and that the application of the luminary has more to do with the actual wooing and events immediately subsequent to marriage.

The following are the probable results of the presence of the planets or lights in the 7th, and the same is to some extent true of their aspects to its ruler :

The Sun........................... A proud, firm-minded partner, with much personality. In the case of women's maps, this delays marriage.

The Moon .... A kind, domesticated partner, but often much change of moods and feelings on both sides.

Mercury .... A quick-minded, intellectual partner, or, if afflicted, a bad-tempered, critical, or nagging one.

Venus .... The marriage is likely to be happy, and the relations between the partners affectionate and a source of joy to each.

Mars .... A strong-minded, and domineering partner. Likelihood of frequent separation, either by quarrels or force of circumstances.

Jupiter .... Prosperity is likely to come through marriage, but it is not always found that this position favours happiness. There is often death and a second marriage.

Saturn............................. Difference of age or station between native and partner. Marriage is late. The partner is likely to be faithful, but often cold or worldly, and engaged on professional considerations to the neglect of wife and home. Narrow affections.

Uranus .... Romantic or tragic conditions in wedlock, according to aspects. The planet is too freedom-loving and forceful to favour happiness in marriage unless aspects are very good. Generally an undesirable significator, unless unusual and unconventional experiences are sought.

Neptune .... Like Uranus, often causes highly unexpected and mysterious events in marriage. Danger of deception, instability, or, in a map of an advanced kind, there may be a platonic union, or one arising from some other form of idealism. Often causes marriage to a cripple or person in some way deformed or injured.

Both Uranus and Neptune incline to extreme sensitiveness, which in itself does not assist towards connubial happiness.

It is necessary to distinguish between positions causing ill-fortune in marriage and those causing actual unhappiness and disagreement. In allying oneself closely to another one assumes, to some extent, their nativities and the good and evil therein, and the closer the union the truer this is. Hence it not infrequently happens that marriage is followed by an abrupt change of " luck ", not always explicable in the light of ordinary common sense. Parts of a natus that have lain dormant may be suddenly stimulated into action. If, for example, a man marries a woman with the Sun applying to the square of Uranus, any element in his horoscope that threatens sudden illness or accidents will be likely to come into action.

On the other hand, happiness in marriage from the emotional standpoint depends on the general suitability of the two horoscopes, their special points of correspondence as explained above, and perhaps more than anything else on Venus. If this is well aspected, especially by the Moon, happiness is probable, irrespective of what the marriage may bring in the way of material trials. Thus, in a case where the Sun applies to the conj. of Saturn and the square of Uranus in the 7th, causing the partner to be consistently unfortunate in business and to suffer from a dangerous and quite unexpected illness soon after marriage, Moon conj. Venus indicated much emotional harmony and happiness.

If, however, Venus be afflicted by Mars we are likely to find tumultuous feelings and little emotional calm or happiness, with prolonged separation ; if by Jupiter, extravagance of feeling, and often lack of sincerity and a restlessness that may easily lead to infidelity ; if by Saturn, jealousy, despondency, and ingratitude ; if by Uranus, an uncontrollable craving for romance and adventures ; if by Neptune, unattainable ideals and consequent unhappiness.

The physical side of marriage comes mainly under the 5th house, and this house also has a good deal to do with the emotions generally. The lord of the 7th in 5th, or *vice versa*, usually shows a love-marriage, or at least one that is not the result of worldly motives. Good aspects between the lords of the houses indicate that marital happiness will be augmented by the physical side of marriage ; and conversely. Heavy bad aspects between 5th and 7th, especially of Saturn, may denote lifelong celibacy. The appropriate luminary applying closely to the bad aspects of Saturn often indicates the same, whereas similar applications to Mars may denote a difficulty in controlling the passions.

With regard to cases where the appropriate luminary separates from an aspect, it is usually the case that this does not cause marriage, but denotes abortive attachments, pleasant or otherwise, according to the nature of the aspect.

The signs, when ascending, tend in varying degrees to produce characteristic fortunes in marriage.

Aries is usually impetuous, warm in feelings, but apt to make a self-willed and obstinate partner. It marries in haste, and probably often repents at leisure.

Taurus rising places Scorpio on the 7th, and this generally causes some danger of illness or death to the partner, and, if not these, at least some form of separation, such as may be due to military or naval service.

Gemini, having Sagittarius on the 7th, often has double attachments or two marriages, or marriage to a foreigner, or one connected with a Jovian occupation. It is often a hardened coquette or philanderer, and is rarely carried away by its feelings.

Cancer is usually a faithful, affectionate, and devoted husband or wife ; there is often a tendency in Cancerian women to marry those who owing to youth or incapacity need " mothering ".

Leo is notoriously unhappy in marriage, despite its warmness of heart and frequent unselfishness.

Virgo, having Pisces on the 7th, nearly always passes through worry and confusion in its love-affairs, frequently becoming involved in some scandal or other trouble. As a partner it is generally faithful and attentive. It rarely marries very early.

Libra is easy-going and readily satisfied ; it takes its emotional adventures calmly, and, although lacking intensity of affection, is easy to live with.

Scorpio has extremely deep and intense feelings ; is liable to jealousy, and although devoted, is often exacting.

Sagittarius generally has several love-affairs, and often two marriages. The feelings are warm but changeful, and without great sympathy or understanding.

Capricorn is little suited to domesticity, and may marry for social reasons or professional ambition, or otherwise subordinate the home-life to the vocational.

Aquarius, although its code of sexual morality is usually its own, so that it is often unconventional and romantic, frequently turns into a very affectionate and sincere partner when once settled in life.

Pisces seems more liable than any sign to plural marriages.

Non-marriage is generally shown by the appropriate luminary making no application at all, and the absence of planets in the 7th house. ♄ afflicting the appropriate luminary or the lord of the 5th may show celibacy.

Indeed, such configurations tend to denote a life into which relations with the other sex hardly enter at all, whereas malefics in the 7th badly afflicted show trouble in such matters.

If the luminary leaves bad aspects of the malefics it also denies marriage, whereas if it applies to such, marriage may take place, or there will at least be love-affairs, but disagreement, estrangement, sickness, or death are likely.

Traditionally marriage is considered much more likely if significators are in the so-called " fruitful " signs, which are the same as the watery trigon. Several rules have indeed been handed down by tradition relative to late and early marriage, as well as numerous aphorisms on sexual matters, but the student is advised to accept these cautiously. They are often interesting, but a clear grasp of principles is of far greater value than a knowledge of any number of isolated rules, exact parallels to which it is difficult to find.

Certain zodiacal areas are found, for reasons not yet understood, to be specially indicative of trouble in marriage and sex-relations generally, if involved in afflictions or occupied by malefics. Thus, 8° Aries-Libra, 25° Virgo, 19° Leo-Aquarius, and 27° Leo-Aquarius.

Horoscopes erected for the time of marriage (see Chapter Eleven, § 2) are often very characteristic of the subsequent course of wedded life.

Friends

As the 5th shows our personal pleasures, so the 11th shows our mental interests, our wishes, hopes, and aspirations, and our friendships.

This house may be judged from the bodies ruling or occupying it, and from these we can form an opinion as to the kinds of friendships the native will make and the course that such friendships will follow, as well as the influence that these will have upon his life.

If the lord 11th be in good aspect with the ruler of the horoscope it shows harmonious relationships with friends; if it be in good aspect with a planet in or ruling the 10th, it shows help from friends and so on.

On the whole the 11th is a fortunate house, and many planets therein, unless badly afflicted, make for success in life.[1]

All clubs, societies, and associations come under it. Lim-

---

[1] On the other hand, the 6th and 12th are, unless well configurated, unlucky, and so, too, in a general sense, ♍ and ♓.

ited liability companies and trade enterprises are probably ruled by the 5th.

§ 3. VOCATION AND FINANCE

Vocation may be judged in a general sense from the whole horoscope and the type of person whom it represents.

Thus a cardinal person needs an active outlet for energy and scope for initiative. A fixed individual will do better in a settled position, with a routine that requires judgment and decision, but not great push or enterprise. A mutable person will do best in a clerical or academic capacity.

In the same way, fire inclines to outdoor occupations ; air, to mental ones ; water, to the sea, the liquor trade, and many everyday occupations ; earth, to agriculture, farming, stock-raising.

The signs have each their special affinities in the world of business and profession :—

Aries .... Engineering, soldiering.

Taurus .... Farming, stock-breeding, cashiers and those who handle hard cash, music.

Gemini .... Journalism, writing, driving vehicles for hire, teaching, Post Office, printing.

Cancer............... Trade of all sorts and shopkeeping, especially in household commodities ; boating and shipping.

Leo .... Stock Exchange, finance, company promoting ; management and control of many kinds, especially in connection with amusements, such as cinemas and the stage.

Virgo. .... Clerical, and secretarial ; medicine, gardening, physical culture, writing.

Libra .... Jewellery, millinery, dress, wine-trade ; often go to sea, brokers and agents of all sorts.

Scorpio.............. Surgeons, sanitary inspectors, chemists, soldiers and sailors, undertakers, butchers, analysts.

Sagittarius .... Religion and the law, professional athletes, publishing, exploration.

Capricorn .... Politics, mining, managerial posts of many kinds, Government employ, labour exchange officials.

Aquarius .... Many intellectual pursuits, such as teaching and lecturing, music and science.

Pisces .... Trades connected with cloth and wool, grocery, footwear sale and manufacture, the sea, painting, welfare work, charities, nursing.

It must be borne in mind that these influences affect the native's personal inclinations when the sign in question is rising, but they may also potently affect the destiny by being on one or more of the three earthy houses. It is in this way that people find themselves forced or drifting into an uncongenial occupation ; the asc. indicates their natural inclination, but some strong sign or planetary position on the 2nd, 6th, or 10th places them in another walk of life altogether. As, for example, a man with Mars and Jupiter rising in Scorpio is made for an open-air life, and would be perfectly at home in the Colonies " roughing it ", but he has Mercury in Virgo on the M.C., and destiny decrees that he must go into a city office, until the force of character shown by the rising sign and planets can assert itself.

Such cases as these are not uncommon, especially when people are born with strong planets in the 12th. Their early life is obscure and their conditions distasteful, but as the planets by progression pass into the 11th and 10th their personal ideals overcome the obstacles denoted by their natal 10th and 4th houses.

When the significators of character are harmoniously placed as regards the vocational houses, a person will find his right path in life.

Great attention should be paid to the strongest planet, for this denotes the category of things most beneficial to the native and most congenial to his own nature. *A strong solar aspect is always very important.*

As regards wealth and success, property, as such, comes under Saturn and most propertied people have this planet either angular, or in aspect to the Sun, or, better still, both. Even bad aspects from Saturn to the Sun are not inconsistent with financial success ; but in this case it will be limited and there will always be danger of loss ; moreover, the position will entail heavy responsibilities.

Venus gives success through the help of others and from personal charm.

Jupiter gives success through good fortune ; and this planet angular, or configured with the Sun, favours success. However, the planet, of itself, does not accumulate, and, if afflicted, indicates loss through over-optimism, gambling, hazardous enterprises, and inordinate generosity. Investments abroad are not likely to succeed and lawsuits should be avoided.

Mars gives fortune by effort ; his good aspects show gain through pluck and hard work.

On the other hand, when much afflicted, he may show hard times of a very bitter sort. Mars, however, has not such a depressing effect as Saturn, and his influence does not seem so interminable or so insuperable. Generally he spends and earns freely, like all fire, while Saturn works slowly and methodically and saves carefully.

Uranian aspects tend to give trouble or benefit as the case may be through government and officials. The native often likes responsibility, and will shoulder it to any extent rather than remain in the background, or be obliged to defer to others, or seek favour with them, or use tact and persuasion. A prominent afflicted Uranus is likely to make any sort of worldly success almost impossible, since the native will be wilful, uncertain in temper, impatient, and perverse.

Neptune, by good aspect, sometimes produces much good fortune, but this has the reputation of being of the nature, often enough, of " fairy gold ", with little substance behind it. It favours success by the sea and, generally, in ♓ occupations (see list above). In bad aspect it occasions worry, trickery, and impracticable schemes.

A careful scrutiny of the 2nd house and the aspects it receives will generally reveal the native's fortune in regard to finance, the good aspects showing whence money will come, and the evil where it will be lost.

The 5th rules speculation, and if this is afflicted, especially in regard to the 2nd, all risky finance should be avoided. Unusual success in speculation is generally denoted by strong good Uranian aspects to the 5th, but even if these are found in the map, they should not be strained too far.

The 6th is important, since it shows what sort of servants the native will have, and whether they will serve him well or dishonestly, and what sorts of faults they will be most prone to commit.

The 7th is involved in all questions of partnership and all kinds of " deals " or negotiation. Hence its value in nearly all business transactions. In this respect, do not judge the nativity as if it were a horary question (see page 197) if the 7th is stronger than the 1st it does not denote that the native will always be worsted in business transactions, but that he will be helped and benefited by partners, and meet honest and generous parties to contracts. If, however, the 7th is very weak he will get no aid from these sources, and if the lord or occupant of the 7th is a malefic and afflicts the ruler of the horoscope, or of the 2nd, he will then lose by contracts and bargains.

The 8th rules all legacies, as well as the partner's money. Thus an affliction between 2nd and 8th would lead to disputes between partners as to money, or loss to one through the finances of the other.

The 10th denotes the social and financial ambitions, which may or may not be realized. It indicates what sort of a figure the native wishes to cut in the world, or, if afflicted, the figure he will have to cut whether he wish to do so or not. It may also denote parental conditions. It is sub-served by the two other occupational houses, representing finance and work, both of which unite to produce that which is denoted by the 10th, i.e., status.

Near the meridian the three fire bodies—Sun, Mars, and Jupiter—all give pride which may incline to arrogance. They tend to a keen sense of personal honour, and, especially in fixed signs, family honour as well. They attract some amount of respect.

Mercury on the M.C. tends to make the native pliable and adaptable, and Venus popular, kindly, and good-natured. Neither planet can be considered strong on the meridian, except in so far as a prominent Venus is always better than a weak one.

These characteristics may affect the selection of the vocation and success therein.

Saturn on the M.C. is a critical position. It gives much responsibility, and, as a rule, much ambition of a persistent kind. If strong it may denote success by merit and perseverance, but it seems liable, if in any way afflicted, to cause ultimate reverses and even downfall. It may denote a similar fate for the father. Saturn weak on M.C. is very likely to indicate a worldly and over-economical parent, and his financial misfortune in old age, especially if it be in Cancer, or afflict the Moon.

Uranus on the M.C. shows many changes of occupation. It inclines either to some unusual scientific profession, such as research, or else to official positions. In any case, the native usually aims at independence of control, and uses original methods. Under affliction the planet may show very heavy misfortunes.

Neptune in the 10th exposes the native to scandal and misrepresentation. It causes the ambitions of the native to be idealistic and unselfish in a good horoscope. In a bad, the imagination may run wild, and the native will involve himself and others in a morass of muddle and illusion. It does not seem to influence the choice of vocation greatly, however much it may affect the native's conduct in the same.

The Part of Fortune is considered by some to have great influence on wealth. This matter has been already discussed (see page 31), and the opinion expressed that such is by no means necessarily the case. It is rather an important centre of self-expression, and necessarily becomes significant of finance in the horoscopes of those whose activities are to a predominant extent directed towards monetary matters.

§ 4. ACCIDENTS AND VIOLENT DEATHS

Liability to accidents is not easily distinguished from liability to disease, and frequently the same aspect will, at different times, cause both.

It may be said that the former are caused by severe afflictions to the hylegiacal points from the malefics Mars, Saturn, and Uranus, especially, perhaps, the first. They are said to be especially likely to cause accidents when on the east side of the map, and when angular and cardinal, but it is doubtful if too much attention should be paid to this, for it is obvious that accidents are capable of considerable differentiation according to their cause (whether the native's fault or otherwise), and according to their special natures. One would expect accidents due to carelessness or lack of foresight or agility to be due to mutable afflictions quite as much as to aspects in cardinals.

Generally speaking, it seems that afflictions from the last few degrees of cardinals are especially likely to cause accidents, but I believe that nativities of victims of accidents are usually characterized by a special prominence of the ends of mutable signs as well. Bodies forming no aspect before leaving the sign they are in are termed " void of course ", and possibly such positions favour accidents.

Mars causes burns, stabbing, cuts, shooting.

Saturn falls, blows, collisions, and crushing.

Uranus explosions, electrocution, and accidents with machinery.

Mars or Uranus in conjunction or opposition to a hylegiacal point are common indications of accidents of a severe kind ; squares seem less common.

149

The four signs ruled by Mars and Saturn, and also Libra, are said to cause violence.

In all cases observe the severity of the affliction and consider how far the benefics may be expected to mitigate it.

Drowning is specially shown by afflictions involving the end of Gemini and Sagittarius, or beginnings of Cancer-Capricorn ; and the end of Aries-Libra and beginning of Taurus-Scorpio.

Murdered persons' nativities generally show violent afflictions in one or more of the following areas : beginnings of the cardinals, about 17° of the cardinals, and the end of the fixed signs (less common).

Those suffering death by judicial sentence generally have a planet (particularly Jupiter) in 17° of the mutables.

Suicides usually have Uranus severely afflicting, especially Mars. Jupiter is generally weak ; there are often few planets in cardinal signs. Mercury and the 3rd are generally afflicted, and common zodiacal areas are 25° of the fixed and about 26° of the mutables.

Poison is connected with Virgo and Scorpio, and Mars and Neptune, while 12° Virgo-Pisces and 11° of the cardinals are common zodiacal areas.

Death in battle is commonly shown by a marked Saturnian element, as well as Martian, and violent afflictions in or near 12° of the mutables are very frequent.

Other kinds of violent death must be studied in the light of general principles applied to each special case. Our knowledge on these matters is in its infancy, but we have reason to believe that, with the growth of scientific astrological investigation, based on statistical research, it is destined in time to become far more precise and reliable.

§ 5. PARENTS AND CHILDREN

The 4th is taken to indicate the father and the 10th the mother, but this allocation has been questioned on the grounds that the Moon, natural ruler of the 4th, is said to signify the mother, and the 10th, corresponding to Capricorn ruled by Saturn, the natural significator of the aged and those in authority, suggests the father.

By some the Moon by night and Venus by day are said to indicate the mother, and similarly the Sun by day and Saturn by night the father. It is possible that none of these bodies definitely stands for either parent. The Moon signifies women generally, and in particular mother and wife, while the Sun stands for men in general, and father and husband in particular, and Saturn is representative of age and authority. The 4th house is the home, and the 10th the public status, and these depend to a large extent, in early life, on the mother and father respectively.

Malefics in the 4th and 10th certainly affect the parents. An opposition between these houses or a bad aspect between the rulers often shows parental disagreement or separation.

The Sun afflicted by Saturn often brings trouble to the father, and, through him, to the native; there may be long illness, business misfortunes, or bankruptcy; or it may show a cold, severe father.

The Moon so afflicted often makes the mother mean, melancholy, selfish or hard, or merely unfortunate and un-

151

able to help the native. On the other hand, benefics with the luminaries or in the two houses bring help through the parents. Indeed, in early life both Sun, Moon and the 4th and 10th operate largely by way of the parents.

Afflictions to the luminaries from Mars threaten the parents with accidents, illness of a Martian type, or immorality. From Jupiter, wastefulness and extravagance. From Uranus, their sudden downfall, or at times insanity. From Neptune, their downfall through muddle or trickery or, sometimes, drink.

The parents' affairs may to a large extent be judged by taking the appropriate house as their 1st, and then proceeding as explained on page 94.

Children are denoted by the 5th, and, to some extent, by the 11th, which is the 5th from the 7th, and so denotes the partner's children. As regards their number, the watery signs are considered most prolific, or " fruitful ", and the fiery (with the possible exception of Sagittarius) and Capricorn the most sterile. The airy signs are average in this respect, Aquarius probably least so. Taurus is more fruitful than Virgo, and is moderately prolific.

Among the planets the benefics, the Moon, and perhaps Neptune are prolific ; the Sun, Mars, Saturn, and Uranus, barren, and the last-named inclines to artificial prevention of conception. Mercury is probably barren, though much influenced by the sign occupied and aspects.

Twins are usually caused by significators in double signs, i.e., Gemini, Sagittarius, and Pisces.

Attention should be paid to planets in the 5th, the sign on the cusp, the position of the Moon, and, in women's maps, the Sun also, while in all cases the ascending sign is important.

The effects of the planets in the 5th may in a general sense be described as follows :—

The *Sun*—few children, but possibility of one being famous or successful.

The *Moon*—increases the number ; they are likely to be commonplace or ordinary in character, unless there are brilliant aspects.

Mercury—clever and intellectual children ; if afflicted, worry through them.

Venus—gifted and affectionate children, and much pleasure through them. They are likely to be well-favoured and popular.

Mars—turbulent and self-willed children ; they are few in number, and are likely to suffer from accidents, if the planet is afflicted. If it has a square from the 8th, danger of their sickness. Separation from children.

Jupiter—prosperous and respectable children, often good at sports.

Saturn—few children, and they are often sickly or unfortunate ; the native feels the responsibility of parenthood heavily ; there may be coldness or estrangement between parent and child.

Uranus—eccentric or talented children ; this planet in the 5th does not favour many children.

Neptune—gives a morbid hatred of children in some cases, and in others an ungratified desire for them. They will be dreamy or artistic.

The signs when ascending have special effects as regards children, due to the nature of the sign then falling on the 5th. Thus, Librans usually make friends of their children, because Aquarius is generally on the 5th when Libra rises, and so on. These secondary influences are often well marked, and the student should exercise his intuition in discovering them for himself.

The sex of the children is judged from the nature of the signs on the 5th, occupied by the ruler of that house, and containing the Moon. Positive (odd) signs are considered masculine ; negative (even) are deemed feminine. In the same way Moon, Venus, and Neptune incline to female children, and the other planets to masculine, except Mercury, which alters according to sign and aspect.

Complete celibacy, in a feminine nativity, or at least childlessness, is most commonly shown by the Sun applying to a conjunction or bad aspect to Saturn, especially in a barren sign, and this is the more certain if the 5th and 7th are involved by occupancy or rulership.

§ 6. TRAVEL

This is connected mainly with the 3rd house, governing short journeys, and the 9th, governing long ones. The distinction usually drawn is that the 3rd rules all journeys that may be completed within the day ; the 9th all longer ones. But it is suggested that the real distinction lies rather in the nature of the journey, the 3rd denoting routine travelling, and the 9th those that bring one into contact with new conditions, partaking to some extent of exploration. Practically the distinction is perhaps not important, as routine journeys are nearly always comparatively short.

Cardinal and mutable signs incline to travel, and so do the planets Mercury and Jupiter, and the Moon. Fixed signs are the reverse, and if these preponderate, especially in respect of the lords of the two houses mentioned, there will be little love of change of abode.

Many planets in Cancer or the 4th give a love of home, and yet there is usually a good deal of moving about in connection with business. The Moon in the vocational houses (2nd, 6th, and 10th) inclines to business journeys. If she rises the same is often the case, and the ruler of the horoscope in the 3rd or 9th, or the rulers of these in the 1st, all tend to bring travel into the life.

The fiery signs all like to get about and see life, especially Sagittarius, and both Libra and Pisces seem often to be wanderers in a physical sense, as well as mentally and emotionally.

A strong 9th, as by benefics or Sun and Moon well aspected being therein, or the ruler strong, makes travelling profitable, and may lead to success abroad, and, if in addition to this, malefics afflict the 4th, the native should leave home and seek a country ruled by the planets strongest in regard to the 9th house and generally.

It is traditionally believed that success may be obtained by settling in a place where one of the benefics at the time of birth was on an angle. Similarly malefics may be removed from awkward positions : a person with a weak malefic exactly on an angle could hardly fail to improve his prospects by removal in any direction !

A careful study of the aspects received by the ruler of the 9th and any planet that may be in it will show the results of travel. Thus a good aspect from the 2nd would show pecuniary benefit, from the 6th benefit to the health, and from the 5th pleasure and enjoyment.

§ 7. RELIGION, MYSTICISM, AND OCCULTISM

Religion and philosophy come under the 9th house, which denotes the mind in its most expansive and explorative aspect, seeking to fathom life's mysteries intellectually. At the same time, since it corresponds to a fiery sign, it possesses faith and hope when manifesting harmoniously.

The Sun in the 9th inclines, generally, to fixed ideas, and it may denote positions of importance in regard to the Churches, but its influence on religious thought depends mainly on aspects and sign.

The Moon inclines to psychic experiences, queer dreams, and, in a weak map, superstitions and vulgar prejudices.

Mercury causes an active, inquiring and sceptical mind, sometimes superficial and flippant. Much depends on aspects.

Venus makes for a poetic or artistic faith with a love of beautiful ceremonies and musical worship.

Mars may cause the native to be a bigot, either on the side of religion or against it, or in low types the native may be completely indifferent.

Jupiter denotes a truly pious, reverent, and philanthropic nature, although bad afflictions may cause formalism, hypocrisy, or a conventional outlook.

Saturn, if strong in this house, makes for profound thought, being intellectual rather than emotional, and favouring either an austere puritanic religion, or a severe philosophy, such as Stoicism. If weak, there is religious depression and fears, fatalism, or hopeless agnosticism.

Uranus here may make an original and profound thinker, or afflicted, an eccentric.

Neptune inclines to such beliefs as Christian Science, spiritualism, or some form of mysticism.

Fiery signs incline, when on the 9th, to religious emotion ; airy to philosophy and metaphysics ; water to occultism on the one hand, or foolish superstition on the other ; earth is often indifferent or formal.

The three houses corresponding to the water trigon rule the hidden, withdrawn side of nature, and many planets therein nearly always incline to some form of occultism, varying in quality, of course, with the general character of the native and the opportunities encountered for rational instruction in such matters. We may thus get abject superstition or profound insight and knowledge.

Uranus and Neptune possess special importance in all horoscopes which we desire to study from the standpoint of occultism, and if these are severely afflicted, much caution must be exercised in regard to such matters, and instruction should only be accepted from teachers of established good faith and recognized sanity of outlook. Otherwise much time and energy will be wasted at the best, and at the worst the native may easily suffer lasting injury, mentally, emotionally, or physically, as the case may be.

It appears that great teachers of occultism frequently have the Sun and Uranus in affliction, but the Moon well placed.

Occultly the influence of Neptune is far more subtle and intangible than that of Uranus, which seems to deal with definite and understandable facts and laws, whereas Neptune induces states of consciousness that possess values beyond earthly measurement, but at the same time are fleeting and not to be constrained.

Astrology has so many sides and there are so many avenues of approach to it, that it can hardly be said that there is a characteristic astrologer's nativity. It appears to come largely under the 9th house in its philosophic and also in its prognostic aspects, for Sagittarius is the sign of prophecy. It is also largely Saturnian, on the positive Aquarian side, while Uranus is considered specially the planet of the astrologer.

It is very common to find planets—especially the Moon, Venus, or Saturn—in or near 27° Leo-Aquarius in the horoscopes of astrologers, and to a less extent in or near 11° Virgo-Pisces.

CHAPTER EIGHT

EXAMPLES OF DELINEATION

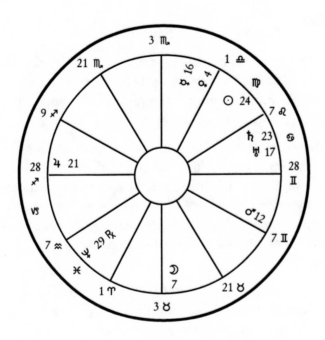

THE above is the nativity of Queen Elizabeth, according to Gadbury, the planets being given to the nearest degrees.

Character.—In this horoscope we find the Elements and the Qualities distributed as follows :

Fire .... Ruler and asc.
Water .... 3 (all malefics)
Air 3
Earth .... 2 (the Luminaries)

These are so well balanced that it would be difficult to choose the strongest.

Cardinal 4
Fixed 1
Mutable .... 4 and asc.

Here fixed bodies are represented only by the Moon, and the Mutable Quality is probably the strongest, showing a flexible and adaptable, but rather fickle and unreliable character.

When we look at the Aspects we can carry this farther. The sun is square Jupiter and opposition Neptune, from which we see that the life would be spent in an atmosphere of intrigue and treachery. The native would be forced—and would indeed probably be quite ready and able—to meet guile with guile. She is described as having had a " love of artifice ".

Mercury in Libra trine Mars in Gemini shows a very quick and acute mind, independent, out-spoken, and sarcastic, but capable of smoothness and charm. Mercury square Uranus shows a " temperamental " and highly-strung disposition, and a despotic, perverse self-willed nature. The square of Mercury and Saturn is weak, but this gives mental narrowness and hardness ; in fact Saturnian afflictions to the Moon and Mercury are common indications of a tyrannical disposition, other things being equal. Mars rules the

3rd house, and is extremely well placed, and this denotes the good education that the princess received, and her intellectual accomplishments and wit. Mercury has a sextile to Jupiter in its own sign, which gave excellent judgment, and must have done much to widen the mental interests. Elizabeth was not indifferent to the science of her times, and the astrologer John Dee received marks of her favour.

Jupiter rising in his own sign is a testimony of an unusual amount of personality ; indeed, it may be said that most people born with a planet rising in its own sign have some degree of personal distinction. (It is noteworthy that King Edward VII also had Jupiter rising in Sagittarius, and the end of this sign on the asc., and a comparison of the horoscopes reveals other notable resemblances.) Elizabeth was in some respects a true Sagittarian ; she was often outspoken, and had bluff and direct moods. But we note that most of the 1st house is occupied by Capricorn, and she had plenty of dignity and aloofness when these qualities were needed. Like Edward VII, she did not tolerate presumption, even on the part of those whom she favoured most.

She was notorious for her meanness. This was probably due to the Lights being in aspect to Saturn (sextile and quintile), and being themselves in earth. Moreover, Saturn rules the 2nd and is in Cancer ; a combination of influences that shows acquisitiveness. Saturn in Cancer is a timid Saturn, indicating prudence degenerated into suspicion and foreboding, which makes the native tend to husband his resources, sometimes beyond the limits both of justice to others and common sense.

Although capricious in personal matters, she was very

tenacious of purpose in regard to national affairs, and this is shown by Saturn conjoined to Uranus in Cancer.

She was extremely vain, and it would be hard to find a map that indicated this trait more clearly. The Sun square Jupiter is a sign of exaggerated self-esteem and personal importance, and, the Sun being in Virgo, this quality was increased by much sensitiveness, to which the Cancerian positions greatly added. Moreover, any Libran element in a horoscope always adds to the approbativeness of the native, this sign being notoriously fond of the approval and praise of others. Again, the Capricornian 1st house influence tends to vanity.

What was the Queen's " evolutionary status ", from the moral and spiritual standpoint ? She had clearly passed, to a large extent, beyond the crude Martian stage, for Mars is " intellectualized " by being in Gemini with good aspects to Mercury. This planet, symbolizing the Intellectual Principle which accompanies man on his journey into matter and finally redeems him, had largely subdued the animal side of Mars. Saturn is less happily placed ; he has good aspects, but is weak by sign, and, as we have said, the moods and fears of Cancer interfere with the true manifestation of the Saturnian virtues of equity, perfect reasonableness and sense, and orderliness. Uranus can hardly be called strong. When we turn to the two benefics we find them both in their own signs, but Jupiter is to some extent vitiated by the square to the Sun and Neptune, and Venus is also opposed to the last-named, without other good aspects, so that neither is very strong. We can hardly find traces of spirituality in the horoscope, but we can probably acquit the Queen of many of the less creditable accusations that have been directed against her, and can say with some assurance that she was beyond the average moral development of her time, whilst without most of the finer qualities of the soul.

Destiny.—The fate of the native in the life of action is shown largely by the Sun, Jupiter, and Mars, and by the fiery signs. Much success can be prognosticated at once from the rising Jupiter in Sagittarius, and the strong Mars, lord of the 10th (although he is cadent), is also a very favourable sign. On the other hand, the Sun is square to Jupiter (lord 12th), and opposition Neptune (in Pisces and natural part-ruler of the 12th), and the progress of the life was hampered and menaced by numerous undercurrents of treachery and plotting. Moreover, the evil planets in the 7th and Mercury lord of the 7th square to them indicate bitter and crafty enemies, and, to some extent, unfortunate or unworthy allies, although the sextile of Jupiter and Mercury, ruling 1st and 7th, denotes some fortunate alliances. The planets in Libra in the 9th show wise councillors. The Sun is in good aspect to Saturn and Uranus, positions that are particularly good for a ruler, and it is to them that her success must have been largely due.

Danger from her near relatives and plots centred on them are shown by Neptune on the cusp of her 3rd house.

The planets in the 7th denote extraordinary and rather sordid relations with the opposite sex, and perhaps this is best exemplified by her affection for the Duc d'Alençon, a disfigured dwarf many years her junior.

She was crowned at the age of twenty-five, when the

M.C. was nearly trine Neptune. At the time of the Armada the Sun was going from trine Uranus to trine Saturn, secondary, and the degree rising at birth was at the M.C. by apparent motion.

Her lonely old age is shown by Saturn, whose influence is strongest towards the close of life. Also by Venus, ruling the 4th opposed to Neptune in Pisces.

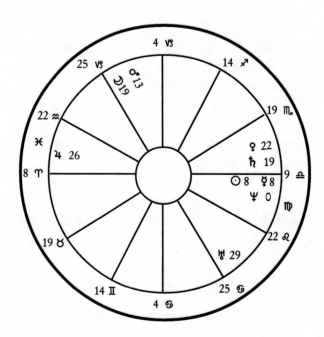

As a second example, contrasting with the first, we give the nativity of the Florentine reformer, Savonarola, the authenticity of which there is no reason to doubt. On the contrary, it is a very clear index to the life and character of the native. The positions are given to the nearest degree only.

Here we find the Venus element very strong, through the sign of Libra, but the external nature, shown by the asc., is Martian, so that we get a rough exterior, but much idealism behind it.

Five bodies are in air, two in earth, and two in water, while the asc. is in fire. One would not expect to find fire the weakest element of the four, but its importance is greatly stressed by the conjunction of Mars with the Moon. It is the horoscope of one who is a dreamer, but who will also come to the front and try to externalize his visions, for Mars always tries to bring things down to the concrete. Moreover, in this horoscope all the bodies except Jupiter are cardinal and most of them angular.

The Moon, conjoined to Mars and square Saturn, must have made the nature austere, fanatical, and turbulent, despite the strong Venus element and the profound sympathies shown by Jupiter in Pisces in the 12th trine Uranus in Cancer.

The position of the Moon also fully accounts for the reformer's desperate struggles with those in authority, shown by Saturn, lord of the 10th. The ruler exalted in the 10th raised him up and enabled him to maintain his position for a time, but Saturn in the 7th (open enemies) and ruling the 11th and 12th (friends and secret enemies) threw him down. It is likely that his friends betrayed him, and it cannot be questioned that he must have resorted too readily to extremes of language, if not of action.

The numerous planets in Libra in the 7th seem to show that the life was largely in the hands of others, despite the vigorous Martian personality. Both Venus and Jupiter are in their own signs, and the nature must have contained much that was sweet and gentle beneath a rough and perhaps un-couth exterior. But the monk was ill-advised, speaking from a worldly point of view, to leave a life of seclusion, for the fiery planets, which have so much to do with all that is public and manifest, are not strong. The Sun is in its fall and conjunction Neptune, without good aspects ; Mars is prominent, but square Saturn ; and Jupiter is cadent and in a watery sign.

The terrible end of the reformer is clearly shown by the afflictions to the Moon.

CHAPTER NINE
PERSONAL APPEARANCE

THE influence of the horoscope upon the physical appearance of the native is one of the most interesting and useful branches of Astrology.

The principal factor in the determination of this matter is the ascending degree, together with all planets in close aspect with it, and the signs containing them.

A planet on the M.C. will also affect the appearance, especially if in aspect with the asc. ; and any satellitium, or group of planets conjoined in one sign, will leave a mark.

The influence of the Luminaries may often be traced, and is sometimes powerfully marked.

A setting planet is important, as being in aspect with the asc., and it occasionally happens that the native's appearance is better described in terms of a setting planet and its sign than by the asc. itself.

Cardinal Signs tend to produce a rather tall, straight, moderately thin body, Aries being often scraggy, Cancer medium, Libra plump, and Capricorn lank.

The head is generally round in Aries and Libra, somewhat longer in Capricorn, but with marked cheek-bones, and rather broad, with a pointed chin, in Cancer.

Fixed Signs produce a heavy, solid build, broad shoulders, and an upright carriage.

The head is usually square, with a strong jaw and chin.

Mutables are inclined to be round-shouldered, often have loose lips and half-open mouths, and, except Pisces, are seldom fleshy.

They have the oval type of face, and usually small chins, but good foreheads.

The typical appearance of the signs may be briefly outlined :

Aries.—A quick, sharp, wide-awake appearance ; there are two distinct types, one with a rather Red Indian physiognomy, the other with a round head, short snubbed nose, and aggressive chin. This type is usually short-sighted and pushes its head forward, wearing pince-nez. The hair is usually reddish, sometimes dark ; the body spare and wiry ; the eyes grey or hazel. The demeanour is energetic.

Taurus.—A slow, deliberate, ponderous manner and a heavy, solid build, inclining to stoutness. The features are good, often there is much beauty of what is called the Irish type. Blue eyes, soft brown hair, red cheeks, and even teeth. The walk is measured, and the whole demeanour of the slow and sure kind.

Gemini.—Generally a light build, with quick, restless eyes, usually brown or hazel. The appearance is often dapper, and indicates intellectuality and mental acquisitiveness.

The demeanour is mobile, discursive, and discontinuative ; quick notice is taken, and then the attention darts to something else. Often nervous.

Cancer.—Often a rather anxious expression, a very kindly and sympathetic smile ; the physical appearance is seldom robust or vigorous, and often the timidity and sensitiveness of the sign is very visible in the appearance, which is rarely " distinguished ". At the same time it varies much with the Moon-position. The eyes are generally light in colour, the complexion and hair pale, the chin pointed, and the nose tilted and also pointed. The eyes are commonly small and deep.

Leo.—This also varies greatly with the solar position. Sun rising in Leo gives a fine, strong, robust man or woman, very broad, large open face and large, rather staring eyes. The complexion is florid and at times apt to be streaked. The hair, as in all fiery signs, inclines to thinness and a light colour.

Other types of Leo are often quite slim and active, and are recognizable chiefly by a long, rather pendulous nose.

Leo has a noticeable liking for dressing in furs, and altogether spends a good deal on dress and appearances.

The demeanour is friendly and jovial, at times self-important.

Virgo.—A neat, precise, scholarly, or clerkly appearance, well formed, and often well set up. The tendency to stoop is less than in the other mutables. The complexion is sallow and often muddy ; the hair and eyes are brown. The demeanour usually impresses one as careful, matter-of-fact, and modestly competent, but the sign sometimes produces a good deal of conceit.

Libra.—Blue eyes, fair hair, and a fair, often pale complexion. The build is moderate in height, slight in youth, and putting on flesh in later life, when there is a marked tendency to develop a blotchy complexion. Sometimes the hair is golden and the eyes very blue at other times the hair is light brown.

The demeanour is sociable, friendly, and happy.

Scorpio.—A thick-set, strong frame ; sallow, olive, or dark red complexion, and hair often black and curly. The nose is prominent and aquiline, and usually thick in the nostrils. Often very muscular. The eyes are dark brown, and often possess a reddish glint. The chin is small but strong, and the face gaunt.

Red- or sandy-haired types, with steel-blue eyes, are sometimes seen.

The demeanour is either reserved and dignified,. or, in low types, surly and rough.

Sagittarius.—Inclined to tallness, athletic, and vigorous, but sometimes stoop. A well-cut, high-bridged nose, fresh complexion, and thin light hair. The face is oval. Eyes grey or blue.

The demeanour is frank, friendly, fidgety, and restless, often with much loquacity.

Capricorn.—Usually tall and loose-jointed. Dark hair, lantern-jawed, long straight nose, white complexion and dark eyes. The beard is always sparse. The skin tends to crease and form folds. At times a peculiar sidelong glance.[1]

The demeanour is either solemn and rather formal, and stilted towards inferiors, or else pushful and anxious to be taken notice of.

Aquarius.—A well-formed, upright build, and handsome open expression ; often very good-looking, but tends to pallor. The cheeks are commonly pinched. Hair light brown, and the eyes either brown or greenish-brown. The head is usually large and square. The demeanour is social, unassuming, and quiet.

---

[1] The text-books usually paint an unprepossessing portrait of ♑, yet handsome examples are by no means unknown !

Pisces.—Often rather heavily and clumsily built, with bright complexion, brown eyes and hair. The features are inclined to be loose and fleshy ; the nose is aquiline, but less finely cut than that of Sagittarius. The eyes are large and protrusive, often bagged. Shoulders are round and the gait rather rolling. Some types are extremely beautiful, and possess much spirituality and a far-off expression ; in lower forms this is represented by a look of anxiety or perplexity.

The demeanour is very subject to moods—alternately full of fun, and then relapsing into depression and worry.

It will be perceived from the above descriptions that the question of personal appearance is a difficult though fascinating one. It is not uncommon to meet fairly typical examples of a sign, but more often a person presents an almost unrecognizable blend from which it is not easy to pick out even one prominent planetary influence. Again, it must be borne in mind that racial heredity necessarily enters largely into the question : a Mongolian is always a Mongolian under whatever configuration he may be born, and in England, where there is a great diversity of racial characteristics, judgment becomes extremely complicated. To get an absolutely pure type it would be necessary to find a person born in a town and country ruled by his own asc. sign, whilst his own nativity should have the ruler rising in its own sign without powerful aspects either to itself or to the asc. degree, and no other sign or planet should occupy a prominent part of the map.

Again, some students lay great stress on decanate influence.

We have also seen that there are often distinct sub-types of signs, which do not seem to depend either on decanate or the position of the ruler, so that it is easy to produce two Leos, for example, that hardly have a visible feature in common, and yet would be instantly identified by an experienced student.

Great attention is due to signs intercepted in the 1st house, especially if they contain planets and the rising sign does not.

The end of a sign on the asc. often produces a fairly true type if the following sign is not tenanted, but when the first one or two degrees of a sign are rising, the preceding sign, which has just left the asc., is often of importance as regards both appearance and character.

CHAPTER TEN

PROGNOSTICATION

§ 1

PROGNOSTICATION involves three classes of planetary positions :

1. *Current*, or those for the actual time in question.

2. *Radical*, or those of the nativity.

3. *Progressed*, or the actual positions of the planets for some time subsequent to birth which are found to operate, according to certain time-measures, at a later time in the life.

These can obviously be combined in several ways. If we denote them by the letters C, R, and P we can get :

1. C + C. These are the different positions taken up by the planets from day to day without reference to any individual horoscope. They do not as a rule greatly affect the individual, but operate through races and masses of people. However, the movements of one's current ruling planet through signs and its passing from stationary to retrograde may produce noticeable effects of a minor character.

   Horary and Electional Figures (see next Chapter) are, of course, derived from current positions, that is, they do not refer to a nativity, but are new figures. They do not lie within the scope of natal astrology at all, for that reason.

2. C + P, and C + R. The passage of any current body over a sensitive point in the progressed or radical horoscope is called a *Transit*. These are of considerable importance.

3. P + R, and P + P. It is by means of these that most prognostication is accomplished. There are two main systems of progression, called Primary and Secondary.

4. R + R represent, of course, the ordinary radical aspects. These may at first sight appear to have no connection with prognostication, but in point of fact no opinion could be more mistaken. *It is a cardinal rule that no direction can bring to pass what is not shown in the nativity.* Exceptions to this are virtually non-existent. The radical horoscope limits the operation of directions inexorably, and the latter only bring to manifestation what is already promised by the former. Hence a real understanding of the radix is a necessary forerunner of all successful attempts to look into the future. The radix shows what will happen ; the directions, when.

§ 2. Transits, Lunations, Revolutions, and the Diurnal Horoscope

The importance of transits varies according to the radical strength of the planets or points involved and the speed of the transiting planet. A slow-moving planet is far more potent than a quick one, such as Mercury or Venus. These latter may, indeed, be as a general rule almost disregarded, but the transits of ♄, ♅ and ♆ are often very significant of events.

The effect of transits is most noticeable when they act as stimuli to a coincident direction.[1] This Law of Excitation, which is one of the most useful and exact in Astrology, may be thus stated :

" *If at the time that a progressed body is in aspect to another by direction, either of these bodies forms an aspect by transit with either of the two directional bodies, then this transit will excite the direction into immediate operation.*"

Thus, if the progressed Sun in 0° Cancer is trine Jupiter in 0° Scorpio, then any transit of the Sun or Jupiter over any point in aspect with 0° Cancer or 0° Scorpio will cause the direction to act.

It will be seen that, according to this statement of the law, the exciting body must be one of the two directional bodies. In our example, a transit of any other body except the Sun or Jupiter would not act as an excitant. This is in accordance with the writer's experience ; excitation by planets other than those in direction is far less certain and powerful.

It will be seen that this law enables the student to determine, often within a day, when a direction will operate. At the same time it explains the frequent concern of beginners

---

[1] Direction is the name applied to the P to P or P to R aspects. Transits are not directions. To " direct " a planet is to move it, according to one of the systems of progression to be explained later, to form an aspect with another.

in Astrology, who find one transit acting with great power and another with very little. The reason is that in one case the transit is a spark that ignites a direction ; in the other it is a spark only.

The effects of transits must be left largely to the intuition. They call into action whatever element in the nativity they chance to touch, but the factors involved are too numerous to admit of the formulation of hard-and-fast rules.

Special attention should be paid to the *stationary positions* of the planets, as, when these fall exactly on a sensitive place in the nativity, important characteristic results will often follow.

Attention should also be paid to *simultaneous transits to the same point*, as when two bodies, in conjunction, are on a radical sensitive point, or two bodies in some other aspect to one another are at the same time in aspect to a radical point. Such configurations vary in importance in accordance with the rules outlined above, but, if very close to the radical place, they deserve attention.

A special class of transits comprises the passage of planets through houses. These may occupy considerable time, from an average of two and a half days in the case of ☽, to an average of fourteen years in the case of ♆. They are often highly significant of the main trend of affairs during the period, so far as the house in question is concerned. If a powerful direction coincides in time and nature, the result will be very marked.

In judging the effect of these transits, much regard must be paid to the radical relationship between planet and house. If, for example, the former were in good aspect with the ruler or occupant of the house in the nativity, the transit through the house would be the more powerful and benefic. If there were no connection at all, it would be far less noticeable.

Mars causes the matters of the house to be active ; the native's attention is drawn to them and his energies directed to that department of his life. Disputes may arise, but progress is also very possible.

Jupiter causes progress, growth, prosperity, and pleasure by its passage through a house, but if badly afflicted at birth there may be loss through overhopefulness, recklessness, waste, and ostentation, or through the matters ruled by the houses over which the planet is lord.

Saturn causes increase of responsibility, even if strong, and brings about consolidation, a settling-down of conditions, or the establishment of affairs on a permanent basis. It may also show hardship, loss, bereavement, and opposition.

Uranus brings unexpected changes, sometimes leading to new conditions of great value, sometimes to loss of time and energy in pursuing false trails, and sometimes to disaster. In mental houses it widens the mind and opens it to new influences and points of view.

Neptune causes chaos, worry, illness, and sometimes treachery, delusive conditions, or moral breakdown. If very strong it may cause gain, something after the manner of Jupiter, and, in watery houses, occult experiences.

The quicker planets do not stay long enough in a house to permit of their effects being very strongly felt. On the other hand, Uranus and Neptune move so slowly that their effects are also not always noticeable, except in long perspective.

Eclipses and Lunations.—These are astronomically the same, except that in the case of an eclipse the Moon has little or no latitude, and so, at the time of ♂ or ☍, it is in a straight line with the earth and sun. Thus, by intervening between us and the sun, it obscures the latter and occasions a solar eclipse, total or partial as the case may be. Or, by passing exactly behind the earth, it is immersed in our shadow, and so suffers total or partial eclipse itself.

An annular eclipse of the Sun is similar to a total eclipse, except that, owing to the Moon's being unusually far from us at the time of obscuration, it is too small to cover the Sun's disc exactly and a ring of light is seen round the lunar orb.

An ordinary Lunation is a new or full Moon, and occurs when the Moon has too much latitude, north or south, to be in a direct line between ourselves and the Sun, and so cause an eclipse.

New Moons are important if they fall on sensitive parts of the nativity or progressed horoscope. Their effects generally appear about four days before the actual day of new moon, and last till the next full moon.

Full Moons are rather less important, but if they fall on a sensitive place their effects will be noticeable.

Eclipses act similarly, but much more powerfully, and, under excitation by a transit, their action may be observed months after their occurrence. Falling on benefics they act well, on malefics ill, and on the Lights, Mercury, or the angles, according to their strength in the radical. It must be borne in mind that an eclipse or lunation is really a simultaneous transit of the lights, and the effects must be judged with due regard to the radical strength of the Luminaries to

one another and to the point or body which they are affecting in the horoscope. If the Sun and Moon are both in
affliction with the radical Jupiter, for example, their conjunction on that body by lunation or eclipse will effect little
good. It would in fact bring into action whatever trouble
the radical afflictions betokened by sign and house.

Ordinary lunations, though not of prime importance,
are well worth watching.

Eclipses, if falling on a radical or progressed planet, may
exert great power and rank equally with almost any direction.

On the other hand, neither lunation nor eclipse will
produce much effect if more than $2°$ from a sensitive point.

They both act as very powerful stimuli under the Law
of Excitation. There can, indeed, be no more potent stimulus of a solar or lunar direction than an eclipse falling on
either of the directional bodies.

It must be noted that what are called eclipses in the
almanac may be invisible in England. Indeed, a total solar
eclipse is a rare event with us. In all cases the greater the
degree of obscuration the more powerful the effect.

Solar and Lunar Revolutions

This is a method of prognostication that has found
favour with some astrologers and was indeed very popular
in the seventeenth century.

A figure cast for the time when the Sun by transit returns to its exact radical place is considered in relation to
itself and to the radix, and is deemed significant for the en-

suing year. The events it foreshadows are supposed to occur when the Sun by transit stirs them into activity.

A similar lunar revolution can be calculated for each month.

Another method is based on the return of the Moon each month after birth to the same distance, or *elongation*, from the Sun, progressing each body. Each of these months is said to equal a year of life. These figures are called Synodical Returns.

To calculate the time when the ☉ (or any other body) reaches its radical place, subtract the log. of its motion in the 24 hours in question from the log. of its distance from that place at noon. The result is the log. of hour and minute from noon when it reaches that place.

The Diurnal Horoscope

This is of recent introduction. A figure is erected for the day under consideration, using the sidereal time of that day and the same time of birth as for the nativity. That is to say, it is erected as if the native were re-born every day at the same hour a.m. or p.m. as was actually the case.

Such a figure, cast for any birthday, will, of course, nearly resemble the radical map so far as the houses are concerned. Then, with each additional day after the birthday, the angles will progress according to the increment in the sidereal time at noon on each successive day.

Such figures are said to be of use in determining the day when a direction will operate, and it is supposed that the coming of a planet on to an angle in the diurnal map will produce marked results.

§ 3. Secondary Directions

It will be convenient to treat these before Primaries on account of their greater simplicity and the fact that they are in much commoner use.

They are based on the rule that *the planetary configurations subsequent to birth produce results in the life according to a time measure of one day equals one year.* That is to say, each day after birth represents a year of the life. Consequently, each hour equals about a fortnight.

It will thus be seen that a slight uncertainty as to the time of birth does not materially affect this system.

Only one difficulty arises, *viz.* What is meant by a " day " ? A *sidereal day* is the time taken by a fixed point, such as a star, to pass from one transit of the meridian to another. A *true solar day* is the time taken by the Sun, which is not stationary and does not move regularly, to do the same. A *mean solar day* is the average solar day, and is about four minutes longer than the sidereal day, because the Sun moves about a degree forward in the zodiac in every twenty-four hours, and so meets the meridian later. The usual method is to use the mean solar, or clock day. The difference between the mean and true solar day does not affect the planetary positions materially, but would alter the houses. The use of the sidereal day would mean that our time-measure would be *one day (sidereal) equals a year and a day*. Therefore we should calculate the time of each direction in the usual manner, presently to be explained, and then add one day for each year of the native's age. The present author considers this to give truer results.

The study of secondaries presents little difficulty. The method is to erect a map for each day after birth, using the new sidereal time for that day and the same time, a.m. or p.m. as the case may be, as was used in erecting the nativity itself. Of course the progression is continuous, and no map will represent exactly more than the moment to which it corresponds in accordance with the time-measure, but by erecting a map for each day (= year) it is easy to see what the intermediate positions will be.

Each successive map will show a progression of the Sun, Moon, and planets, and also the M.C. will advance about one degree, whilst the other houses will also advance, as shown in the table of houses for the place in question.

The progressed bodies will all form directions, from time to time, to other progressed bodies (since they all move at different rates) and to the various radical positions. Thus we have P to P and P to R directions, of which the latter are usually the more marked in action.

It may be observed that some writers on Secondaries (or, as they are sometimes called, Arabian directions) do not move the houses at all from their radical positions, arguing that such movement, being due to the axial rotation of the earth, is in reality primary. The system taught here is properly known as *The Progressed Horoscope*, and is a popular and convenient method which unites the whole of the Secondary System with important elements (i.e., the progression of the angles) from the Primary.

Let us now consider, as an example, a person born in London at 6 p.m., January 1, 1924.

We erect the nativity. The S.T. at noon on day of birth = 18° 39' 30" to which add 6 hrs. min., which gives a radical M.C. of 11° 0' Aries.

Now, from the moment of birth, the planets and houses move. If we want to see how they stand after one day, i.e., one year of life, we erect a map for 6 p.m. on 2nd January. The S.T. is now 0 hr. 44 min. 26 sec., or a progression of 3 min. 56 sec., which gives an M.C. of 12° 5' Aries, while the planetary positions must all be recalculated, and, except Neptune, who is retrograde, have all moved forward.

We continue erecting similar maps for each day after birth.

The tabulation of directions must now be considered. These may be classified as follows :

- *a.* Aspects formed by the Sun p. to all bodies p. and r. and to the asc. and M.C. r.
- *b.* Aspects formed by the asc. and M.C. p. to all radical bodies.
- *c.* Aspects formed by all p. bodies except the Lights and Angles to the radical Lights and Angles.
- *d.* Interplanetary aspects p. to r. and p. to p.
- *e.* Aspects by the Moon p. to all bodies p. and r.

Of these *a* and *b* are most important and cover the chief events and stages of life. Owing to their comparatively slow motion they are not numerous, and can be soon tabulated.

c. These are usually less important, especially directions to radical angles.

d. These are omitted by some writers, but this attitude is not recommended. At the same time mutual or interplanetary directions, as they are called, often effect little unless an appropriate Lunar direction concurs.

e. These are of great importance. In themselves they do not indicate the main events of life, but if they concur with one of the other four classes they denote the exact time of action. By themselves they last from a week to one or two months, according to the nature of the aspect and the radical strength of the bodies.

Aspects formed by the progressed Sun or angles are often significant of lasting epochs in the life and may extend their influence over two or three years, coming into marked operation when excited by transits or secondary lunars.

Directions to progressed positions are sometimes said to be less powerful than those to radical, but this may well vary with the individual, and the student should form his own opinion.

Students often ask for instruction as to how directions will work out, but beyond the general rule that *they tend to bring to fruition all that is foreshadowed in the radical map* it is almost impossible to go. The rest must be left to intuition and experience. It is the writer's opinion that it is almost impossible to make forecasts from directions with anything like precision unless one is extremely well acquainted with the character, habits and circumstances of the person in question. The astrologer is in the position of a physician who can only make forecasts when he has thoroughly examined the patient's constitution and studied his reactions. One may of course make " lucky hits " but this will not satisfy a scientific astrologer.

In order to see during which month a direction becomes exact, it is only necessary to do a short sum.

1. If the direction is to a radical position, find how far the moving body has to go to make the aspect exact, using minutes. Multiply this by twelve and divide by its daily motion, also in minutes. The result gives the months after the birthday when the direction is exact. If, instead of twelve, you take 365 you get your answer in days.

Example.—In the case given on page 182, when will Sun ✳ Mars r. be exact ? Mars r. = 18° 25' ♏, so that ☉ must reach 18° 25' ♑. On the 9th, at 6 p.m., it is at 18° 13' ♑; therefore it has 12' to go, and its daily motion is 61'.

Then 12 x 365 = 4,380, which divided by 61 gives about 72. It will, therefore, become exact about 72 days after the 8th birthday.

2. If the direction is to a progressed (i.e., moving) body, we must find out how much the directed body gains on the other in a day. Unless it does gain, it obviously cannot form the aspect at all. Then find out how much it is behind the complete aspect.

Then say : If it takes a day to gain so much, how long will it take to gain what it needs to complete the direction ?

Example.—On January 23, 1924, at noon, the Sun is in 2° 13' ♒ and ♂ in 2° 23' ♐ , and we see that at noon on the next day the Sun has passed the sextile. When was this ☉ ✶ ♂ exact ? Now the Sun's motion = 61', and Mars' = 39', i.e., the Sun gains 22' in the day. And at noon it is 10' from the exact aspect.

If it gains 22' in the day (= dir. year) it will obviously gain 10' in 10/22 of that period.

We have selected a birth-time at noon for simplicity's sake, but that in no way affects the method.

After a little practice all times, except the Moon, can be detected to the nearest month by mere inspection of the ephemeris.

With the Moon it may be thought advisable to tabulate its monthly position by adding one-twelfth of its daily motion to its birthday position for each successive month. This enables aspects and the month of their being exact to be more readily detected.

185

It is often advisable to reckon lunar directions to the exact day by the foregoing method, using 365 instead of twelve, and so obtaining the answer in days.

Example.—On January 2, 1924, the Moon is conjunction Mars p. : when does this fall ?

$$\text{Moon's motion} = 882'.$$
$$\text{Mars' motion} = 38'.$$

Therefore Moon's gain in day = 844'.
Moon is behind by 208'.

Then, if it gains 844' in 365 days, in how many will it gain 208' ?

$$\frac{365 \times 208}{844} = 90 \text{ days}$$

Lunar directions often produce their maximum results very punctually on, or just before, their exact date.

The student should adopt a methodical style in calculating directions, and should take them exhaustively planet by planet.

An excellent plan is to form, once for all, a table of your Places of Aspect. Go through the natus carefully, tabulating every point which is in any aspect (you can omit quintiles and other minor aspects if so desirous) with any planet. Then, when wishful to discover if any progressed body is near any aspect with the radix you need only glance at your table, and, provided it has been correctly drawn up, any oversight or omission is impossible. The initial labour is saved many times.

Progressed directions (p. to p.) are not shown in this way, but are given in modern ephemerides.

Parallels are things apart, but can be worked out by the

foregoing method, although perhaps they are best dealt with by means of a *graph*.

For this purpose procure squared paper and write in the degrees of declination, from 0° to 25°, on the left hand, with perhaps 2 lines between each, for thirds of a degree. Then let the vertical lines represent your birthdays for successive years. Again leave some lines between these for subdivisions of the year, according to the scale on which you wish to work.

Then, in red ink, rule across the sheet the radical declinations of each body, marking beside each what it is. If two bodies have the same declination one line will serve for both. These lines will be exactly horizontal, since the radical dec. remains unaltered.

Then, in pencil, plot the annual progressed declinations of each body. The Moon will form sharp curves, but the others will alter very little, and probably very regularly, so that you need hardly plot them for each year. Uranus and Neptune will deviate very little from their radical line.

Wherever two lines intersect, a progressed par. dec. aspect is shown, and the vertical line will indicate the time of operation, more or less exactly according to the scale of the graph.

By these means the par. dec. aspects of a lifetime can be tabulated in an hour or so.

Those who are fond of such methods can extend them to other branches of Directional Astrology. It is easy to make a graph that will show all p. to r. directions, for instance, but not p. to p.

The Adjusted Calculation Date

This is a labour-saving device well worth mastering.

Refer to the example on page 182.

Since birth was six hours (= a quarter of a day) *after* noon, noon itself must correspond to a quarter of the year, or three months, *before* birth. It will, therefore, be perfectly legitimate to work always with the *noon positions*, copied straight out of the ephemeris without any calculations, at the same time dating everything not from the birthday, but from an Adjusted Calculation Date, which is to the birthday as noon is to the time of birth.

Thus if a person were born at noon his birthday and A.C.D. would coincide ; if he were born two hours before noon, noon would equal one month after the birthday, and so on throughout the twenty-four hours.

This, of course, applies to the Sun, Moon, and planets, but not to the houses, which (unless adjusted) will continue to refer to the real birthday.

Pre-Natal Secondary Directions

These are calculated in exactly the same manner as ordinary post-natal secondaries, but are reckoned backwards instead of forwards, so that the twenty-four hours immediately *before* birth corresponds to the first year of life, and so on.

They have, as a rule, less value than post-natals, and the beginner can safely disregard them.

They are not known to differ as regards the *kind* of influences which they indicate from ordinary post-natal directions, although theories have been advanced on the subject.

Planetary Periods

At this point it is appropriate to mention the fact that each planetary influence tends to be active at a certain period in human life rather than at others. This scarcely belongs to the study of directions properly so-called, and yet it often explains the sweeping changes that sometimes come over a person's fortunes, and, to some extent, the disposition as well.

The Moon rules infancy. As the child learns to run and talk he comes under Mercury, and this persists till puberty or later, gradually giving way to a greater or less extent to Venus. This is followed about the age of 22 by the period of the Sun, when the native takes his place in public life and begins to make his mark in life, if at all. Then comes the Mars period, from 41 to about 56. Then that of Jupiter, when the purely physical activities of the Sun and Mars begin to wane, and the mind and emotions are broadened, whilst the life settles down to comfort if the earlier activities have been successful. Lastly, Saturn rules from about 68 onward into old age.

Uranus is thought by many to rule extreme longevity. Neptune rules senility.

These periods vary greatly according to the nativity. A very Saturnian person will be dominated by that planet all his life, for good or ill as the case may be. But its clearest manifestation will be during the Saturnian period, and so with the others.

§ 4. PRIMARY DIRECTIONS

These are based on the *apparent* motion of the heavenly bodies immediately after birth, no account being usually taken of their proper motion.

The time-measure is the passage of one degree of right

ascension over the mid-heaven of the horoscope, which is taken to equal one year of the life. As one degree passes over the M.C. in about every four minutes of time, it will be seen that this measure is very rapid, and a slight error in time will throw many of the directions out by many months. For example, twenty seconds equal a month. The rapidity of the measure also explains why no notice is generally taken of the *proper* motions of the planets: ninety years of life only equal six hours of time, and in this period most of the planets move very little. Nevertheless it seems that account may be taken of the proper motion of the Moon, and even of the Sun, Mercury, Venus, and Mars, and direction may be made logically and successfully both to their radical and progressed positions.

Primaries are considered to denote above all matters of fate or destiny, while having small influence on the development of thought and character. They are therefore of great importance in judging accidents and other matters over which the native has little or no control.

Their calculation involves time and care, and more than the average aptitude for mathematics, and their consideration is usually included only in the more advanced grades of text-books. Yet their importance forbids their entire omission.

It is usual to calculate only those primaries that involve what are called the Significators, i.e., Sun, Moon, M.C., and Asc. These are directed, or moved, to the places of other bodies, or to the places of degrees in aspect to other bodies or to the significator itself. Thus, we have always a *preceding* body or place of aspect, which is considered as remaining stationary in its radical place in the heavens, and we have a *succeeding* body or place of aspect which is brought to it.

Thus, in Queen Elizabeth's map the place of Saturn may be assumed to stand still, and the Sun is directed to it. This would be styled, in conventional phraseology, Sun conj. Saturn *converse zodiacal*, so called because the Sun is moved in a direction contrary to the sense of the zodiac. On the other hand, we could bring Mars to the place of the Moon, and this would, very misleadingly, be called Moon conj. Mars *direct zodiacal*, it being feigned that in this case the Moon has moved to the place of Mars in the sense of the zodiac.

All ordinary primaries are really converse, because they are formed by apparent motion, which is always converse to the zodiac.

In the same way, the Moon passes to the radical places of 4° and 16° ♈, and is then opposition Venus and Mercury, by so-called converse direction.

Interplanetary primaries are effective, but are not always used.

The coming of bodies or places of aspect on to the angles gives us directions to these points, and these are easily calculated. Thus when Jupiter, in Elizabeth's map, comes on to the M.C., we get what is called M.C. conj. Jupiter, although Jupiter, being the moving body, ought to be written first. In the same way when 4° ♑ arrives on the M.C. it will be square Venus.

In order to reckon primary directions to the M.C. it is only necessary to get a table showing the R.A. corresponding to the zodiacal degrees, such as is to be found in Sepharial's *Directional Astrology**, and then to convert into R.A. the radical M.C. and the degree of the place of aspect.

191

* Retitled **Primary Directions, A Definitive Study**, and reprinted, 2006, by Astrology Classics. — *Publisher's note*

The difference will give the arc of direction, which turn into time at the rate of one year for each degree and one month for each five minutes.

To calculate the asc. is harder, but this may be correctly done by finding the R.A. of the M.C. when the place of aspect rises, and then directing the radical M.C. to this second M.C. as if it were an M.C. direction. Thus to calculate the arc for asc. conj. Neptune in Elizabeth's map, find the R.A. of the M.C. when 29 Pisces rises, and then subtract radical R.A.M.C. from it. Needless to say, for these directions positions must be taken to the minute.

Solar primaries seldom differ much in point of time from the corresponding secondaries, but lunar primaries are a class by themselves. Calculation of these two classes of primaries, as well as of inter-planetaries, is made by a proportional sum involving the semi-arcs and meridian distances of the two bodies and worked by logarithms.

The student is recommended to study primaries in such works as Robson's *Text-Book*, Zadkiel's *Grammar* (reprinted with Lilly's *Introduction*), and the before-mentioned work of Sepharial, but unfortunately many differences of opinion exist as to theory and practice, and the whole subject is embarrassed by a very arbitrary terminology.

§ 5. SYMBOLIC DIRECTIONS

By this term are denoted all directions not based on any astronomical motion of the planets or houses.

Such directional methods have been in use since antiquity, but they have recently received renewed attention by reason of the introduction of fresh measures by W. Frank-land and by the present writer, whose *Symbolic Directions in Modern Astrology* deals with the subject in detail.

These measures have the advantage of extreme simplic-ity, and, although they have not been before the astrologi-cal public long enough to be fully tested, they appear at least as satisfactory as the more difficult systems.

In all symbolic methods there is a fixed annual incre-ment or progress, which is added to all factors, including the angles.

The principal measures are :

The *Radix Measure*, introduced by Dr. Gornold, which is the mean daily motion of the Sun (and is therefore not, in the fullest sense, symbolical). This motion is 59' 8" a year of direction and tables are published to show the progress by this ratio in any number of years and days.

The present writer has found an annual increment of 1^0 to be, not only much simpler to use, but equally or more accurate. Thus, for 20 years of life we add 20^0 to all factors, 5' corresponding, of course, to a month.

A much slower measure is ¼ ^{0} to the year. This seems to affect worldly prosperity and status, favourably or unfavourably according to aspect. It is liable to indicate serious illness or even death. For 20 years the increment would, of course, be 5^0, and so proportionally for other ages.

Frankland introduced a measure of 4/7ths of a degree per annum, and this seems very effective and valuable. To apply this it is only necessary, if it is desired to find the age at which a direction will operate, to multiply the arc by 7 and divide by 4. Thus, if two bodies are 20⁰ apart, they will be conjoined, by this measure, at 35 years. But if it is desired to know what the arc for any age is, then multiply the age by 4 and divide by 7. Thus, at age 21 the arc is 12⁰.

The same writer has introduced the *Point of Life*, an imaginary point which, starting in all maps at 0⁰ ♈, progresses through the zodiac at the rate of 4 2/7⁰ a year, or seven years for each sign, forming directions.

The present author has introduced the *duodenary* measure of 2½⁰ a year, and the *subduodenary*, which is one-twelfth of that distance, or 12' 30". To use the subduodenary measure, reduce your arc to minutes, multiply this by 8, and divide by 100—this gives the age at which it will eventuate. Thus, when will a direction 10⁰ apart become complete ? 10⁰ equals 600' ; multiply by 8 = 4,800 ; divide by 100, and the answer is 48 years. To find the arc for any age, multiply that age, in years and decimals of a year, by 100, and divide the result by 480. Thus, if the age is 38.4, multiply by 100 = 3,840, and divide by 480 = 8⁰.

These measures may be tested on Queen Elizabeth's nativity.

§ 6. Rectification

When the time of birth is not known, or is known only approximately, it is customary to endeavour to *rectify* the horoscope, or in other words to adjust it to a putative correct time.

If the hour is not known even approximately it may be possible to perform a rough rectification by considering the physical appearance, temperament, and fortunes of the native, a map for the day of birth being moved to and fro until it appears to conform to these data.

For example, if the native has undergone many unexpected financial losses Uranus may be moved into the 2nd, and a general examination will ensue as to how far this agrees in other respects with his life, as, for instance, does the condition of the 7th agree with his marriage experiences ?

When a satisfactory preliminary adjustment has been made (or if the time has been approximately recorded) the determination of the exact time of birth is comparatively simple.

This is usually done by the passage of planets over the angles by primary direction, as explained on pages 191, 192. This method, however, is only possible in the case of adults.

We may see that our hypothetical map puts Jupiter in the 10th house, about 12° of R.A. from the M.C. We then ask : Did any event transpire about the age of 12 which would be in conformity with such a direction as M.C. ♂ ♃? If we find that it did not, but that such an event happened two years later, then we move the M.C. 2° back, and test again by some other direction. The more events we can use in this way, the better ; and finally we strike an average from the several results we have obtained, so as to get the M.C. which gives the best mean result.

As time goes on a hypothetical time can be constantly tested, until it becomes practically certain.

The slower symbolical measures (particularly the subduodenary) are extremely useful for rectification.

For example, in the writer's nativity Saturn is 4⁰ 42' west of the M.C., which, by the above measure, equals 22 years, 11 months and a few days. This exactly coincided in time and nature with an event of great importance, thus confirming the birth-time, which had previously been rectified to the foregoing M.C., from recorded time, by primary measures.

The Pre-Natal Epoch is often used for purposes of rectification, and is highly esteemed by some practitioners ; but this branch of astrology is beyond the scope of the beginner.

Indeed rectification of any kind requires judgment and experience.

CHAPTER ELEVEN

HORARY AND ELECTIONAL HOROSCOPES

§ 1. Horary Questions

HORARY Astrology is that branch of the science by which the student obtains an answer to any question from a figure of the heavens erected for the moment at which the question is first put to him, or, if it is a personal affair, for any time at which he finds his mind specially exercised about it, and the impulse comes to him to try to obtain a solution by casting a figure.

It will be seen that Horary Astrology is particularly useful to those who are ignorant of their birth-time, since data of this kind are not needed. The figure is cast in the ordinary way for the place where the student is at the time. It is also in other respects simpler to understand and practice than Natal Astrology, and from a practical point of view it is often of more use, since by its means a definite answer may be obtained to a definite query.

Horary Astrology has been practised from very early times. It was particularly favoured by the Arabs and flourished greatly through the Dark and Middle Ages to the detriment of the other aspects of the science. William Lilly, in particular, brought it to great perfection at the time of the Protectorate and Restoration, and his works have been a mine of material for later books on the subjects. In recent years a tendency has arisen to relegate it to a position of less importance, and the fact that it has been largely used for trivial or self-seeking purposes has obscured its philosophic interest and real value.

The figure being cast as explained, it is necessary, before proceeding to judge it, to ascertain whether it is *radical*, that is to say, a genuine figure upon which judgment can be based. As a rule, all figures cast in a serious spirit and with a clear idea in the mind of the questioner of what he wants to know are radical, but it is probable that the personal element enters into this, especially so far as figures cast about the student's own matters are concerned. A person in whose horoscope Mercury or Jupiter is heavily afflicted should be cautious in judgment as to the future, especially when his directions or transits to these afflictions are evil. Moreover, note that a malefic exactly rising or setting often renders a figure unsafe to judge, and it is also generally necessary to withhold an opinion if the beginning or end of a sign, say within 3°, is on the asc. Such conditions as a rule indicate a confused state of mind on the part of the questioner.

The personal appearance of the *Querent* (i.e., Questioner) may also be compared with the asc. (which always denotes the person putting the question) with a view to seeing if there is a correspondence such as one would expect. Early astrologers paid much attention to this, as a means of telling whether the map was radical, and it may be that in this manner the basis of zodiacal physiognomy was laid. Much notice was also taken of moles and scars, as it was found that these occur on that part of the querent's body ruled by the rising sign and by the sign containing the ruler in the horary figure ; the same is true of the 6th and its ruler, and very often of the sign containing the Moon and the two malefics, especially if these aspect the rising degree. Names and clothes were also taken into account, for certain ascendants undoubtedly favour special names, colours, and fashions.

The figure itself, however, usually bears the clearest indications of its own radicality, which experience, but only experience, will teach the student to discern. The ruler, Moon or Part of Fortune, will be found in an appropriate sign or house, or the lord of the house governing the matter asked about (called the *Quesited*) may be rising.

Judgment really amounts to this : The asc. and Moon denote the querent ; the quesited naturally comes under one or other of the houses. We thus have three significators, to which may be added ⊕ (of the importance of which, at least in this branch of Astrology, there is no doubt whatever). If these are strong by house and sign and in good aspect, the matter will progress well, or, in technical language, " be brought to perfection ".

Significators in angles and cardinal signs will denote a rapid course of events.

The ☽ or ⊕ heavily afflicted nearly always spells great delay or an altogether negative outcome of the matter, whilst they assist greatly if they are well placed and aspected.

If the significators come to a conj. or good aspect easily, without *frustration* (i.e., first meeting a bad aspect from another body), the matter will come to perfection. If they apply by bad aspect the matter is likely to end in a quarrel, separation or loss, unless the significators are otherwise very strong, when the outcome, may be satisfactory after numerous failures, by dint of great effort or the use of considerable resources. If the significators separate from an aspect, it denotes the end and dwindling away of the matter, at least for the time being.

Note, however, that *mutual reception*[1] between the significators is of great importance, and indicates an harmonious attitude between them.

House-position is also very important, apart from aspects, and if the lord of the asc. be in the house ruling the quesited, it is a favourable sign, for such a position seems to point to the planet holding control over the things of the house.

Refranation is the turning back of a significator by retrogression before completing an aspect. This indicates that the party indicated will retire from the transaction.

Translation of Light occurs when the significators are not in aspect, or separate from one, and a third swifter planet passes from the aspect of one to that of the other. This indicates the intervention of a third party, useful or otherwise as the aspects may signify.

This may also occur through *Collection*, which arises when a third weightier body, which is received by each of the significators in one or more of their dignities, receives the light of both in turn.

It will be observed that much of this traditional teaching has the flavour of superstition, but experience teaches us that it is true.

A special time-measure is used in Horary Astrology, but it is of rather doubtful validity, and the student may

---

[1] That is, each body in the sign of the other.

find that he can judge this more accurately by attention to the actual time in which the significators form subsequent aspects, bearing in mind what might seem reasonable under the circumstances of the case. Suppose, as in the example given below, a quickly moving significator of the querent is within a few degrees of the trine to that of the quesited, the rest of the horoscope showing no impediments. Then three times are suggested for the perfecting of the matter : when the trine is exact ; when the next sextile is exact ; when the conj. is exact. Usually it is possible to tell from the circumstances of the case which is the most likely.

The orthodox time-measure is to take the number of degrees necessary to complete the aspect between the significators, and to count them as follows, according to the position of the applying body :

Cardinal Sign and angular House	= days.
Cardinal Sign and succeedent "	= weeks.
Cardinal Sign and cadent "	= months.
Fixed Sign and angular House	= months.
Fixed Sign and succeedent "	= years.
Fixed Sign and cadent "	= indefinite.
Mutable Sign and angular House	= weeks.
Mutable Sign and succeedent "	= months.
Mutable Sign and cadent "	= years.

The following table is used in order to determine direction, as when desiring to trace lost property.

1st House, East
2nd House, E.N.E.
3rd House, N.N.E.
4th House, North.

5th, N.N.W.
6th, W.N.W.
7th, West
8th, W.S.W.

9th, S.S.W.
10th, South.
11th, S.S.E.
12th, E.S.E.

♈, East
♉, S. by E.
♊, W. by S.
♋, North.

♌, E. by N.
♍, S. by W.
♎, West.
♏, N. by E.

♐, E. by S.
♑, South.
♒, W. by N.
♓, N. by W.

EXAMPLE

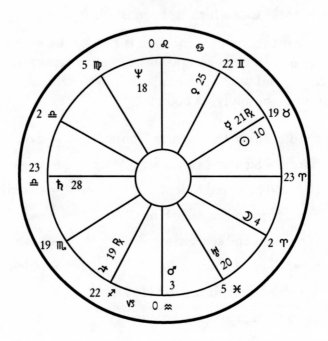

The question in this case was as to the time of delivery of a motor-car, much overdue. It is given here because it shows particularly clearly what is meant by radicality. The question obviously refers to a 3rd house matter, and to one in which delay ($\hbar$) is involved. Saturn, part-lord of the 3rd, rises in a cardinal sign, and Venus, lord of the 1st in Gemini, the third sign, goes to the trine of Saturn. Mercury is retrograde, but goes to the sextile of Uranus. The Moon, though cadent, is cardinal and without bad aspect. The car, as might be expected, arrived two days later when Venus was exactly trine Saturn.

Needless to say, figures are not by any means always so easy to judge, for the matter asked about may be complex, and so may be the solution of the affair.

§ 2. ELECTIONS

The term " horary " is often loosely applied also to maps that are not cast in answer to a question, but for the moment when something of the nature of an inception or beginning takes place. For example, we have maps for the time of marriage, for signing a deed, the striking of a bargain, the commencement of a battle, or a declaration of war. These are often wonderfully significant and interesting, and it is to be noted that logically they are of the same category as an ordinary nativity ; they are, indeed, nativities. In order to distinguish them from horary questions it is proposed to call them " *Inceptions* " .

When these inceptional figures are the result of deliberate choice made with a view to obtaining favourable astrological influences for the undertaking, they are styled " *Elections* ".

These have long been considered an important part of astrology, and although it is an open question as to how far a favourable election can override a bad nativity, yet it seems reasonable to believe that it may help to do so. This does not disprove astrological teaching, for the judgment used by an astrologer in choosing a favourable time for himself, or the prudence shown by a non-astrologer in seeking astrological advice on such a matter, are themselves the fruits of some good natal aspect, which works out in this very manner. It is often found, however, that the man who elects a good time for some undertaking of a nature which his nativity does not favour, will either be prevented from using the time elected for that purpose, or else will have already suffered from the difficult natal position, and, thanks to astrological knowledge, is now able to escape its action to a greater or less degree.

Very little information on elections is now obtainable in printed form,[1] but it can perhaps be summed up in the following: Elect a time when the current horoscope would supply a favourable answer to a horary question as to the success of the matter to be begun.

Let the Moon, the Part of Fortune, the asc., the ruler, and the house ruling the matter be as strong as possible.

Sometimes it is necessary to consider two or even three or more houses ; thus, if we wanted to consider a time suggested for beginning a cycling holiday abroad with a friend, we should need to regard 1st, 3rd, 5th, 9th, and 11th.

Since it is extremely hard to find a perfect figure, it is suggested that a strong Moon and a rising benefic will probably be the two items that it would be well to try to secure.

---

[1]Since this was written, an excellent book by V. E. Robson has appeared on the subject.

When under bad directions it will often be found extremely hard to make good elections. On the other hand, when under good directions, there is less need to bother about them ; they will fall into line with the stronger influence. Nevertheless, even then a good election would probably add strength to the direction.

Note that the Moon is considered weak in horary and electional figures when " *void of course* ", that is, forming no aspect before leaving the sign she is in.

CHAPTER TWELVE

THEORETICAL CONSIDERATIONS

WE have now discussed the practical side of Natal Astrology in its entirety, and seen how the nativity is erected, progressed, and judged. The thoughtful reader will, however, find these studies not only interesting and useful in the highest degree in themselves, but also an extraordinary incentive to further and deeper investigation and thought.

It is not difficult to see that the phenomena of astrological science are different from those of physics, chemistry, and other branches of human knowledge which deal only with physical matter. It is true that many astrologers do seek to explain astrology in terms of physics. For example, the facts of wireless telegraphy are used as a basis for illustrating the nature of the influences which produce (as this school claims) the results known to astrology. But it seems clear that astrological facts are different from these. Sometimes we seem to encounter examples of direct effects, as for instance when a transit of Mars causes us to cut our finger, to lose our temper, or to act in some way on impulse. But how shall we explain, by any analogy drawn from physics, the equally indisputable fact that often a similar astrological indication results, not in our *doing* anything, but in our *becoming the objects* of the actions of others ? Thus, we may (to continue the above illustration) be cut by the careless act of another, be assailed by an individual who, through no behaviour of ours, has lost *his* temper, or suffer from the impulses of another. Again, there are the facts of directional and horary astrology, which, it is considered, point to something very different from the natural laws known to physical science. Another peculiarly interesting and radically important doctrine of astrology is the supreme significance of the *beginning of anything*, whether this law operates in respect of the nativity, of an inceptional figure, or in horary astrology.

Another school of astrologers attempts, to some extent, the explanation of astrological science by means of theosophy and kindred schools of occultism, though I am not aware that any efforts have been made from this quarter to give a comprehensive explanation of our problems.

This much must be universally conceded, that man, whether he is part of the Cosmos or is a distinct principle planted in it, as in a field for development, is certainly affected by it and in turn is able to act upon it. From the standpoint of self-development it would obviously be without purpose to place man in the Cosmos unless this reciprocal action were possible.

But we do not call all the effects of the Cosmos that man encounters astrological ; if he is soaked by the rain or drowned in the sea we do not call the action of rain or sea an astrological effect, but a purely physical one. Astrology, however, would give a sufficient reason why any individual, at any particular time, is brought into contact with the rain or with the sea, unless the results of such contacts were so trivial as to defy investigation.

Hence it seems that Astrology is the science of certain subtle or occult relationships, which cannot be interpreted in terms of physical science, and cannot even be readily brought within the conception, fundamental in physics, of causation. For what astrologer knows whether the planets cause, or indicate, events, or whether their action is not something beyond such ideas altogether ? If they do actually cause events, then they operate in a manner different from that of physical causation.

A man dies, let us say from the effects of injuries incurred years before, and Saturn comes at the time of death to the conjunction of his son's mid-heaven. That conjunction could have been calculated long before the father was injured, but it did not happen till the father had died a death that had become inevitable long before. How then could the transit be said to have been the *cause* of death ?

What physical analogy is there to the marvellous manner in which various appropriate directions coincide in the horoscopes of numerous people at a time when something happens to affect them all ?

It is known, by the experiments of qualified scientific investigators, that there is a realm, call it what we will, in which phenomena take place that cannot be explained in terms of physical science—I refer to the phenomena usually called " psychic ". I believe that the operations of the planets belong primarily, though not necessarily entirely, to that sphere, which is of a different order from the order of physics.

In this sense astrology may be justly called an occult or cryptic science.

THEORETICAL CONSIDERATIONS

When we turn, however, to the significance of the astrological factors, as distinct from the way in which they actually affect us, we reach a higher plane, and are dealing with Symbology. For the Sun, Moon, planets, signs, houses, and aspects unquestionably derive their meanings from cosmic principles, as I have endeavoured to explain elsewhere.[1]

With respect to the old question—Can a man rule his stars ?—it is abundantly true that the influence of the planets is exceedingly penetrative, and the man who tries, by any ordinary means, to avoid a bad direction, has a difficult task before him. For, whatever precautions he takes, it always seems as if the direction finds an open door somewhere through which to discharge its effects.

Common sense would appear to indicate the reasonableness of taking ordinary care when directions are evil, and to make appropriate use of good influences. No one, unless incredulous as to the truth of astrology or wilfully careless, would choose to take a sea-voyage under an evil Neptunian direction ; though it is fairly certain that such prudence would not entirely defeat the direction.

Besides taking such reasonable steps, various schools of thought have suggested means to nullify planetary influences. For example, talismans, amulets, and similar devices are used by many.

It is probable that courage and faith are more valuable than any such means, and that these, in fact, are valueless without such inner supports. The cultivation of such attitudes of mind stimulates the benefic action of Jupiter in our

---

[1]*The Zodiac and the Soul*, published by The Theosophical Publishing House.

maps, and, if they do not remove tribulations, at least they help us to bear them.

Thus, though man cannot " rule his stars " in the sense of manipulating or twisting their effects to his own ends, he can and should lift himself above the sphere of their action by those methods which the great moralists of all time have inculcated. If the student places his true good in his intellect and reason he will not concern himself unduly over mundane success or failure, and he will try to lift others to the same elevation of thought. It is only the part of man that belongs to Nature which is susceptible of planetary effects but " there is a principle of the soul superior to all Nature, through which we are capable of surpassing the order and system of the world " (Iamblichus).

Man cannot, perhaps, conquer the stars upon their own plane, but he is, by the intrinsic dignity of his being, superior to this plane ; and he can at any time and at all times lift himself above its ever-changing surface by the exercise of the spiritual faculties of his soul. This is the true " ruling of one's stars ".

It is also the solution of the problem of fatalism so often raised in astrological discussion. For when man sees in all that happens to him or to others the irresistible tide of Providence, willing and accomplishing the highest good of all beings, he then consciously and gladly unites his will to the Divine Will : thus the seeming conflict between freedom and fate is finally resolved.

BIBLIOGRAPHY

IT is suggested that the student who wishes to acquire a sound astrological library at moderate cost might advantageously begin with the purchase of the following :—

NATAL ASTROLOGY

1. What is a Horoscope and How is it Cast ? By Alan Leo.
2. The Horoscope in Detail. By Alan Leo and H. S. Green.
3. 1001 Notable Nativities. By A. H. Barley.
4. Student's Text-book of Astrology. By V. E. Robson. 7s.
5. Encyclopaedia of Psychological Astrology. By C. E. O. Carter.
6. The Astrological Aspects. By C. E. O. Carter.

DIRECTIONAL ASTROLOGY

7. Directions and Directing. By H. S. Green.
8. Directional Astrology. By Sepharial.
   Also No. 4 above, and Zadkiel's Grammar, reprinted with No. 11.
9. Symbolic Directions in Modern Astrology. By C. E. O. Carter.

MEDICAL ASTROLOGY

10. Raphael's Medical Astrology.
    No. 5 above (Specific Diseases).

THE PRINCIPLES OF ASTROLOGY

HORARY ASTROLOGY
11. Introduction to Astrology. By W. Lilly.

THEORETICAL ASTROLOGY
12. The Reason Why in Astrology. By H. S. Green.
13. The Zodiac and the Soul. By C. E. O. Carter.

MUNDANE ASTROLOGY
14. Mundane Astrology *and* Weather Predicting. Both by H. S. Green.

GENERAL
15. New Dictionary of Astrology. By Sepharial.

INDEX

213

INDEX

INDEX

INDEX

BOOKS ON ASTROLOGY
by CHARLES E. O. CARTER

●

AN ENCYCLOPAEDIA OF
PSYCHOLOGICAL ASTROLOGY

With observations on the astrological characteristics of about fifty diseases and an introductory essay on the zodiacal signs. Third edition revised and enlarged.

SYMBOLIC DIRECTIONS IN
MODERN ASTROLOGY

Symbolic Directing occupies but a fraction of the time required for the measures in common use.

THE ZODIAC AND THE SOUL

A treatise on the most profound aspects of astrology ; it reveals in clear language the essential Ideas that arc portrayed in the symbols of Astrology.

THE ASTROLOGICAL ASPECTS

One of the most helpful books that have appeared in recent years, containing an entirely original study of the values of the various astrological aspects, based on a large collection of actual cases.

SOME PRINCIPLES OF HOROSCOPIC
DELINEATION

Containing Ten Chapters on the Scope of the Nativity : —The Aspects—Mundane position—Sign position—Planetary Psychology—Infant Mortality and Longevity—Suicide and Insanity—The Violent Criminal—Outstanding Ability and Failure.

Better books make better astrologers.
Here are some of our other titles:

AstroAmerica's Daily Ephemeris, 2010-2020
AstroAmerica's Daily Ephemeris, 2000-2020
 - both for Midnight. Compiled & formatted by David R. Roell

Al Biruni
**The Book of Instructions in the Elements of the Art of
 Astrology**, *1029 AD, translated by R. Ramsay Wright*

Derek Appleby
Horary Astrology: The Art of Astrological Divination

E. H. Bailey
The Prenatal Epoch

C.E.O. Carter
An Encyclopaedia of Psychological Astrology
The Principles of Astrology, *Intermediate no. 1*
Some Principles of Horoscopic Delineation, *Intermediate no. 2*

Charubel & Sepharial
Degrees of the Zodiac Symbolized, *1898*

H.L. Cornell, M.D.
Encyclopaedia of Medical Astrology
 958 pages, hardcover, the ultimate astro-medical reference

Nicholas Culpeper
**Astrological Judgement of Diseases from the Decumbiture of
 the Sick**, *1655, and,* **Urinalia**, *1658*

Dorotheus of Sidon
Carmen Astrologicum, *c. 50 AD, translated by David Pingree*

Nicholas deVore
Encyclopedia of Astrology

Firmicus Maternus
Ancient Astrology Theory & Practice: Matheseos Libri VIII,
c. 350 AD, translated by Jean Rhys Bram

William Lilly
Christian Astrology, books 1 & 2, *1647*
   The Introduction to Astrology, Resolution of all manner of questions.
Christian Astrology, book 3, *1647*
   Easie and plaine method teaching how to judge upon nativities.

Alan Leo
The Progressed Horoscope, *1905*

Claudius Ptolemy
Tetrabiblos, *c. 140 AD, translated by J.M. Ashmand*
   The great book, in the classic translation.

Vivian Robson
Astrology and Sex
Electional Astrology
Fixed Stars & Constellations in Astrology

Richard Saunders
The Astrological Judgement and Practice of Physick, *1677*
   By the Richard who inspired Ben Franklin's famous Almanac.

Sepharial
Primary Directions, a definitive study
   A complete, detailed guide.

Sepharial On Money. *For the first time in one volume, complete texts:*
   • **Law of Values**
   • **Silver Key**
   • **Arcana, or Stock and Share Key** — *first time in print!*

James Wilson, Esq.
Dictionary of Astrology
   From 1820. Quirky, opinionated, a fascinating read.

H.S. Green, Raphael & C.E.O. Carter
Mundane Astrology: *3 Books, complete in one volume.*
   A comprehensive guide to political astrology

If not available from your local bookseller, order directly from:
The Astrology Center of America
207 Victory Lane
Bel Air, MD 21014

on the web at:
http://www.astroamerica.com

LaVergne, TN USA
22 November 2009

164992LV00003B/6/P